ROANOKE COUNTY AND THE ROANOKE VALLEY

▪▪ TURNING THE CENTURY ▪▪

Editorial coordination by Dan Smith
Written by Dan Smith, Christian Moody, and Christina Koomen Smith
Featuring the Photography of Douglas Miller
with Contributing Photography by Dan Smith

Produced in cooperation with the
County of Roanoke

CELEBRATE 2000 PHOTO CONTEST WINNERS

Winners' images can be found throughout this book and also in a special section beginning on page 104.
Congratulations to all our winners!

ROANOKE COUNTY AND THE ROANOKE VALLEY

▪▪ TURNING THE CENTURY ▪▪

Editorial coordination by Dan Smith
Written by Dan Smith, Christian Moody, and Christina Koomen Smith
Featuring the Photography of Douglas Miller
with Contributing Photography by Dan Smith

ROANOKE COUNTY AND THE ROANOKE VALLEY

TURNING THE CENTURY

Produced in cooperation with the County of Roanoke

Editorial coordination by Dan Smith
Written by Dan Smith, Christian Moody, and
Christina Koomen Smith
Corporate profiles by Judy Siegel, Sharon Gnau,
Laurel Holder, Amy L. Shelor, and Christina Koomen Smith

Featuring the photography of Douglas Miller
with contributing photography by Dan Smith

Community Communications, Inc.
Publisher, Ronald P. Beers

Staff for *Roanoke County and the Roanoke Valley:
Turning the Century*

Acquisitions:	Henry S. Beers
Publisher's Sales Associate:	Jim Sparks
Editor In Chief:	Wendi L. Lewis
Managing Editors:	Angela C. Johnson & Lenita Gilreath
Profile Editor:	Amanda J. Burbank
Design Director:	Scott Phillips
Designer:	Matt Johnson
Photo Editors:	Angela C. Johnson & Matt Johnson
Print Production Manager:	Jarrod Stiff
Contract Manager:	Christi Stevens
National Sales Manager:	Ronald P. Beers
Sales Assistant:	Sandra Akers
Acquisitions Coordinator:	Angela P. White
Proofreaders:	Heather Ann Edwards & Carolyn Phillips
Editorial Assistants:	Krewe Maynard & Eleanor Planer
Accounting Services:	Stephanie Perez
Pre-Press and Separations:	Artcraft Graphic Productions

CCI

Community Communications, Inc.
Montgomery, Alabama

Chief Executive Officer:	David M. Williamson
President:	Ronald P. Beers
Chief Operating Officer:	W. David Brown

COVER PHOTO BY DOUG MILLER.

Table of Contents

PHOTO BY DOUG MILLER.

FOREWORD

This was a moment that occurs every 40 generations or so—that point in time when all the zeros fall together to create a millennium. Roanoke County approached the year 2000, oft referred to as Y2K, with excitement, anticipation, and some trepidation just as most other governments and businesses did. Would our computer systems and equipment accommodate the change in dates? Would our businesses and citizens be prepared? Looking beyond the turn of a century and millennium, were we prepared for the future?

Despite dire predictions, we felt confident and ready. We wanted to enjoy this historic time. We wanted to preserve the past and, at the same time, run into the future as a leader in technology, education, and medical opportunities. Most of all, we wanted to celebrate the people and places of Roanoke County.

As part of our celebration, we held events remembering our past and entertaining our families, hosted a balloon festival and a technology show, and sponsored a photo contest, which is featured in this book. Throughout the year 2000 and into 2001, we made new plans and faced new concerns. We left the century that saw the invention of automobiles, televisions, and personal computers and moved forward into the unknown and unimaginable.

This book is a snapshot of life here at the turn of a new century and a new millennium. It will serve as a reminder to future generations of this moment in time in Roanoke County, Virginia, and a reminder to us of the fun we had in celebrating a once in a lifetime experience.

—Elmer Hodge
County Administrator

PREFACE

Of all the good that can be made of living in the Roanoke Valley, none is so dear to me as that it is a wondrously comfortable place to fall in love.

The reasons to live in this mountain-draped haven are infinite and growing. They read, even from the most calloused native, like a litany from the Chamber of Commerce.

I've been here since 1971 and never seriously considered moving, although my hometown, Asheville, North Carolina, is often considered to be one of the best places in the country to live.

Everything I want is here. I've raised two children here, and the opportunities the Roanoke Valley provided them were simple, direct, and full of potential.

When I was approached to organize this I leaned on two people I knew (Judy Siegel and Christian Moody) and one I didn't: Christina Koomen, a woman whose writing impressed me. She was also a Roanoke native, who'd gone off to school in Charlottesville and stayed for 20 years. Over the months we became close friends, a couple of what she calls "fun junkies." She found she missed being in Roanoke; she missed home. Then, a funny thing happened: we fell in love. And we got married. And we had a book.

Here's the book.

I sincerely hope you enjoy reading it as much as we enjoyed making it.

—Dan Smith
Editorial Coordinator

PART ONE

PHOTO BY DOUG MILLER.

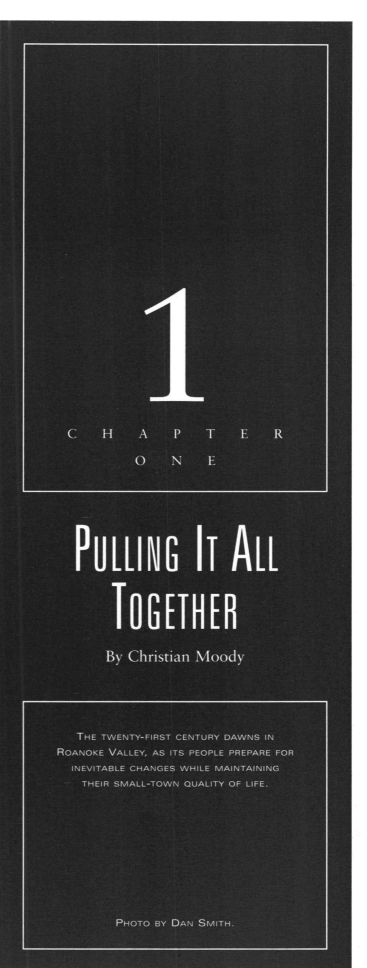

1

C H A P T E R

O N E

PULLING IT ALL TOGETHER

By Christian Moody

THE TWENTY-FIRST CENTURY DAWNS IN
ROANOKE VALLEY, AS ITS PEOPLE PREPARE FOR
INEVITABLE CHANGES WHILE MAINTAINING
THEIR SMALL-TOWN QUALITY OF LIFE.

PHOTO BY DAN SMITH.

When people discuss Virginia's system of local governments, the Roanoke Valley is a self-contained case study. The Roanoke River gently flows through one county, one town, and two cities, home to about 225,000 people. Roanoke County surrounds the cities of Salem and Roanoke. In Virginia, cities are independent from counties. The Town of Vinton is within Roanoke County, but is governed by an elected town council and mayor. The town provides some services within its limits, such as public safety and road maintenance, while the County provides others, including schools and libraries.

About 97,000 of the Valley's residents live in the City of Roanoke, which was chartered in 1884. Roanoke changed its name from Big Lick in 1882, and grew into an urban center, chiefly on rail power. The predecessor of the Norfolk & Western Railway opened shops and a rail yard in the late nineteenth century. It is governed by an elected mayor and city council, who appoint a city manager to oversee general operations.

Salem, founded in 1802 east of an estate owned by Revolutionary War General Andrew Lewis, was located on the western turnpike. When the first town charter was drafted, settlers had only been in the valley about 60 years. Salem remains a center for many Roanoke County services, but voted to become an independent city in 1967. On January 1, 1968, the City of Salem was born, causing the County to lose a bit more than 14 square miles of land to the new locality. Salem is governed by a mayor and city council, though the mayor is chosen by the members of council rather than being directly elected by the voters. Salem also uses the city manager form of government.

Roanoke County's board of supervisors is similar to a city council, setting policy for the overall operation of the County. The County is divided into five magisterial districts—Hollins, Cave Spring, Windsor Hills, Catawba, and Vinton. A member of the board is elected from each district, and represents approximately 16,000 citizens. A chairman is elected by the board members on an annual basis, and the day-to-day overseeing of county operations is handled by an appointed county administrator who supervises the staff which carries out the policies set by the board.

Roanoke County provides many services to its citizens which are unusual for a county of its size. In 1990, after a referendum by the voters, the County created a police department to provide law enforcement. Shortly thereafter, the department became one of the first in the southwest part of Virginia to receive accreditation from the Commission on Accreditation for Law Enforcement Agencies (CALEA). The Fire and Rescue Department provides services including advanced life support and modern firefighting operations through a combined system of volunteer and career personnel. All households in the County, whether located in a housing development or on top of a mountain, receive weekly curbside garbage pickup, with additional bulk and

ROANOKE COUNTY WELCOMES YOUNG AND OLD TO THE AREA AND INVITES THEM TO EXPLORE THE BEAUTY AND HISTORY FOUND IN THIS EXCEPTIONAL PLACE TO LIVE, WORK, OR SIMPLY VISIT. PHOTO BY DOUG MILLER.

ABOVE: COUNTY OFFICIALS
WORK IN THE MODERN ROANOKE
COUNTY ADMINISTRATION
BUILDING OVERSEEING THE DAILY
OPERATIONS OF THE LOCAL
GOVERNMENT, INCLUDING THE
PARKS AND RECREATION
DEPARTMENT, SOCIAL SERVICES,
INFORMATION TECHNOLOGY,
AND LAW ENFORCEMENT
DEPARTMENTS. PHOTO BY
DAN SMITH.
LEFT: THE ROANOKE COUNTY
COURTHOUSE AND JAIL,
LOCATED IN SALEM, HOUSES
BOTH MALE AND FEMALE
ADULT INMATES. PHOTO BY
DAN SMITH.

RIGHT: THE REGION'S HISTORY IS RECAPTURED IN EXHIBITS FROM THE ICE AGE THROUGH MODERN DAY AT THE HISTORY MUSEUM AND HISTORICAL SOCIETY OF WEST VIRGINIA. PHOTO COURTESY OF CENTER IN THE SQUARE.

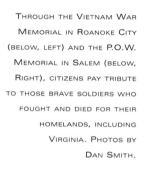

THROUGH THE VIETNAM WAR MEMORIAL IN ROANOKE CITY (BELOW, LEFT) AND THE P.O.W. MEMORIAL IN SALEM (BELOW, RIGHT), CITIZENS PAY TRIBUTE TO THOSE BRAVE SOLDIERS WHO FOUGHT AND DIED FOR THEIR HOMELANDS, INCLUDING VIRGINIA. PHOTOS BY DAN SMITH.

brush service available on a reservation basis. Spring Hollow Water System, featuring a 3.2-billion-gallon side-stream reservoir with a 243-foot roller compacted dam and a state-of-the-art water treatment plant, provides public water to thousands of residents, and also is interconnected with the City of Roanoke's water system to position the local governments to provide service during water emergencies.

Roanoke County libraries were the first in the Valley to provide Internet access for patrons, and the Parks and Recreation Department has active programs for senior citizens, teenagers, the physically challenged, and youth athletics.

Additionally, the County has joined with the other Valley governments to provide efficient service to the citizens. Examples of regional cooperation include the wastewater treatment plant, a regional fire and rescue training facility, the Roanoke Regional Airport, a government and educational access television facility, and the juvenile detention center. The Smith Gap Landfill, located in Roanoke County, and the Tinker Creek Transfer Station, located in the City of Roanoke, are connected daily by the Waste Line Express, operated by Norfolk Southern.

For Roanoke County, change is the operative word of the past half-century. The County has been transformed from a rural collection of small, unincorporated communities clustered around the best agricultural land to a suburban haven for nearly 84,000 residents. In 1986, Roanoke County became the first county in Virginia to be chartered.

In recent years, Roanoke County has concentrated on building a technological and industrial base in its new commerce and industrial parks. It has sought industries like R.R. Donnelley, one of the most successful book printers in the world, which provides well-paying, high-quality jobs for Valley residents. ■

ABOVE: SPRING HOLLOW WATER SYSTEM, FEATURING A STATE-OF-THE-ART WATER TREATMENT PLANT, PROVIDES PUBLIC WATER TO THOUSANDS OF RESIDENTS, AND ALSO IS INTERCONNECTED WITH THE CITY OF ROANOKE'S WATER SYSTEM TO POSITION THE LOCAL GOVERNMENTS TO PROVIDE SERVICE DURING WATER EMERGENCIES. PHOTO BY DAN SMITH.

LEFT: ORIGINALLY KNOWN AS WOODRUM FIELD, ROANOKE REGIONAL AIRPORT SERVES WESTERN VIRGINIA FROM COMMERCIAL AIRLINES AND FREIGHT CARRIERS TO PRIVATE AVIATION AND THE MILITARY. PHOTO BY TOMMY FIREBAUGH.

ROANOKE COUNTY ENVELOPS ITS
RESIDENTS BY PROVIDING
NECESSARY SERVICES INCLUDING
LAW ENFORCEMENT, FIRE AND
RESCUE SQUADS, AND GARBAGE
PICKUP. PHOTO BY
DOUG MILLER.

THE LARGEST DEPARTMENT OF ITS KIND IN VIRGINIA, THE ROANOKE COUNTY FIRE AND RESCUE DEPARTMENT IS DEDICATED TO PROTECTING THE LIFE AND PROPERTY WITHIN THE REGION OF ITS 12 STATIONS THROUGH A COMBINED SYSTEM OF VOLUNTEER AND CAREER PERSONNEL. PHOTO BY GEORGE WARNER.

BELOW: THE WASTE LINE EXPRESS, OPERATED BY NORFOLK SOUTHERN, IS PART OF A COLLABORATIVE PROJECT BETWEEN SEVERAL LOCAL COMMUNITIES. THROUGH THIS UNIQUE SYSTEM, HOUSEHOLD GARBAGE, COLLECTED AT THE TRANSFER STATION, IS HAULED TO A COMMON LANDFILL BY TRAIN. PHOTO COURTESY OF ROANOKE VALLEY RESOURCE AUTHORITY.

ABOVE: SALEM OFFICIALLY
BECAME AN INDEPENDENT CITY
ON JANUARY 1, 1968,
YET RESIDENTS STILL ENJOY
THE PEACEFULNESS OF A
SMALL-TOWN SETTING.
PHOTO BY DAN SMITH.
RIGHT: A WELL-TENDED ROSE
GARDEN IS LOCATED ADJACENT
TO SALEM'S CITY HALL.
PHOTO BY DAN SMITH.

THE TOWN OF VINTON IS
WITHIN ROANOKE COUNTY
AND PROVIDES SOME SERVICES
WITHIN ITS LIMITS, SUCH AS
PUBLIC SAFETY AND ROAD
MAINTENANCE, WHILE THE
COUNTY PROVIDES OTHERS,
INCLUDING SCHOOLS AND
LIBRARIES. PHOTO BY
DOUG MILLER.

2

CHAPTER

TWO

THE CULTURE CLUB

By Dan Smith

ANNUAL FESTIVALS INCLUDING THE CHOCOLATE
FESTIVAL, VINTON DOGWOOD FESTIVAL,
STRAWBERRY FESTIVAL, ROANOKE FESTIVAL IN
THE PARK, BLUE RIDGE GARDEN FESTIVAL,
SALEM FARMERS' MARKET BLUEGRASS
FESTIVAL, AND CHILDREN'S FALL FESTIVAL
ARE PART OF THE CULTURE AND
HERITAGE OF ROANOKE.

PHOTO BY DOUG MILLER.

While there is little argument that the Roanoke Valley is the hub of commerce, transportation, banking, education, and government for the western half of the state, it is in arts and entertainment that the area shines.

Consider this. The Valley has more than 30 movie screens, with another 16 being built as the century turned; two major theatrical groups; two ballet troupes; a number of theme museums (transportation, local history, art, theater, science, nineteenth-century frontier society); centers for crafts and creative arts; the venerable Thursday Morning Music Club; a storytelling association; a large and storied bluegrass and old-time music club; a significant writers' conference along with several writers' clubs, as well as an artists' league; a large and prestigious symphony orchestra; a regional opera company; a national touring chamber music ensemble in residence at Roanoke College; and various arts organizations with significant outreach elements for the education of school children and the community at large. These offerings constitute a rich and diverse mixture of opportunities for the citizens of Roanoke County.

Roanoke County has been important to the success of the Valley's cultural organizations. Mill Mountain Theatre, for example, saw 60,000 people attend its theatrical productions during the 1998-99 season, and 40,200 of them were from Roanoke County. Nearly 1,000 of its season

ticket-holders were from Roanoke County, and there were 776 Roanoke County students who attended matinees through Mill Mountain Theatre's Theatre in the Schools program. The Mill Mountain Players took its professional traveling troupe's full productions to seven Roanoke County schools during the year and exposed 2,323 students to live theater, all the while satisfying a portion of the students' state-mandated Standards of Learning criteria.

Mill Mountain Theatre's board of directors lists half of its 30 members from Roanoke County, and 130 of its 201 Drama Enrichment program (acting classes for middle school and high school students) are from the County.

Center in the Square, meanwhile, was host to a total of 7,687 Roanoke County student visits at its resident organizations during the 1999 fiscal year, and its outreach programs served 5,168 more students.

County residents are central to the operations of each of the Center in the Square organizations, volunteering and donating large sums of time and money to keep the arts alive and thriving in an era of diminishing government support at the national, state, and local levels. Area arts organizations have adjusted to sometimes severe losses of government allocations with resourcefulness, often bordering on genius. Those separate entities, generally competitors for a limited supply of philanthropic funds in the past, have increasingly learned to work together, to pool resources, and to have considerably more impact in tandem.

THE SCIENCE MUSEUM OF WESTERN VIRGINIA ALLOWS VISITORS THE OPPORTUNITY TO EXPLORE THE WONDERS OF SCIENCE AND NEW TECHNOLOGY THROUGH INTERACTIVE EXHIBITS. PHOTO COURTESY OF CENTER IN THE SQUARE.

ABOVE: MILL MOUNTAIN THEATRE IS ONE OF THE BASES OF A LIVELY THEATER TRADITION THAT ATTRACTS PEOPLE FROM ALL OVER THE WESTERN PART OF THE STATE. *PINOCCHIO* WAS ONE OF THE IMMENSELY NOTABLE PERFORMANCES THIS PAST YEAR AT MILL MOUNTAIN. PHOTO BY DAN SMITH.

LEFT: ANOTHER OF THE AREA'S POPULAR THEATERS IS LOCATED AT HOLLINS UNIVERSITY WITH SEVERAL LIVE PRODUCTIONS EACH YEAR. HOLLINS THEATRE RECENTLY PERFORMED *GOOD OL' GIRLS*. PHOTO BY DAN SMITH.

Virginia's Explore Park in east Roanoke County is a living history museum focusing on life along the Great Wagon Road. The park recently saw its link to the Blue Ridge Parkway completed and expected 2000 to be a record year for visitors wanting to take a trip to an 1840s working village, complete with blacksmith shop, tavern, church, and all the elements that made for a civilized settlement 160 years ago. Even the livestock and foliage are period-appropriate, and Explore Park has taken advantage of its perch along a pristine portion of the Roanoke River to house workshops, nature studies, and a mountain-bike trail.

Mill Mountain Theatre and Showtimers, which together are nearly 100 years old, are the base of a lively theater tradition that attracts people from all over the western part of the state. While Mill Mountain's two theaters are the center for professional production in the region, Showtimers offers the lively tradition of community theater with several productions a year. In addition, Hollins University, Roanoke College, and two civic centers offer live productions throughout the year.

Music rings out from parks, bars, clubs, civic centers, churches, and just about any other place where two people can gather. Roanoke County is part of a festival center for the region, and music is integral to that endeavor. County residents are deeply involved in the Roanoke Symphony Orchestra, Opera Roanoke, the Southwest Virginia Ballet Company, Roanoke Ballet Theatre, the Fiddle and Banjo Club, the Chorus of Sweet Adelines International, the Southwest Virginia Songwriters Association, and more garage bands, Celtic music groups, bluegrass ensembles, and rock 'n' roll quartets than you can threaten with a drumstick.

Roanoke County school children are among the beneficiaries of the region's heavy emphasis on the arts. Center in the Square, for example, is not only host for touring school classes at the Science Museum of Western Virginia (complete with planetarium), but Mill Mountain Theatre also produces classics studied by high school-age students (often with young actors from County schools) and children's theater programs for the younger ones. In addition, a number of arts organizations actually visit the County's schools with presentations ranging from science and theater to history.

Polish and culture dot the Roanoke Valley in small pockets. The Kandinski Trio at Roanoke College is one of the foremost chamber ensembles in the United States; the Greene Memorial (United Methodist Church) Fine Arts Series is a simply superb series of six major music events each year; the Virginia Gentlemen Barbershop Harmony Society of Roanoke performs regularly at Cave Spring High School; and the Harrison Museum of African-American Culture preserves the heritage of an unique people. Also located in the Valley are WVTF Public Radio, one of the most successful public ration stations in the country, as well as WBRA Public TV, one of the oldest public television stations in the state.

Roanoke County's parks and recreation department and libraries have been increasingly active in the arts in recent years. The parks department has sponsored cultural heritage, storytelling, and music festivals at Green Hill Park while the libraries continue to be wellsprings of activity, providing Internet access in addition to a full range of traditional tools.

The Arts Council was a leader in the effort to elevate the arts to a front-burner position in the community, emphasizing the importance of its economic development at the Cultural Summit 2000, which was held in April at Hollins and featured nationally known speakers. Those efforts appear to be gaining strength among business and government leaders who realize that, with an economy dramatically changing in post-industrial, technological America, where a person lives has less to do with holding a job—in a technological society you can live where you want and work from a computer— and more to do with the quality of life available. ■

ABOVE AND LEFT: THE BEAUTY AND HISTORY OF THE DOGWOOD TREE IS OBSERVED EACH YEAR AS VENDORS AND RESIDENTS FILL THE STREETS OF ROANOKE COUNTY WITH MUSIC AND FESTIVITIES FOR THE YOUNG AND THEIR PARENTS. CHILDREN ENJOY CRAFTS WHILE ADULTS TAKE PART IN SPORTS ACTIVITIES. PHOTOS BY DOUG MILLER.
FAR LEFT: MILL MOUNTAIN ZOO IS JUST ONE OF THE DIVERSE ATTRACTIONS THAT ROANOKE RESIDENTS CAN ENJOY THROUGHOUT THE COUNTY, CITY, AND VALLEY. PHOTO BY TOMMY FIREBAUGH.

CENTER IN THE SQUARE ON THE HISTORIC FARMERS MARKET, HOME TO MUSEUMS OF ART, HISTORY, AND SCIENCE, AS WELL AS LIVE PROFESSIONAL THEATRE, DANCE, AND OPERA, WELCOMES VISITORS FROM AROUND THE WORLD AND HOSTS GROUPS LARGE AND SMALL. PHOTO COURTESY OF CENTER IN THE SQUARE.

ABOVE: THE ROANOKE
SYMPHONY ORCHESTRA,
FOUNDED IN 1953, IS THE ONLY
PROFESSIONAL ORCHESTRA IN
VIRGINIA WEST OF RICHMOND.
SINCE 1986, THE RSO HAS
BEEN RECOGNIZED IN THE
UNITED STATES FOR ITS
ARTISTIC ACHIEVEMENTS,
INNOVATIVE EDUCATION
PROGRAMS, AND DIVERSE
AUDIENCES. PHOTO COURTESY
OF THE ROANOKE
SYMPHONY ORCHESTRA.
LEFT: A NEW ADDITION TO THE
ART MUSEUM OF WESTERN
VIRGINIA IS ART VENTURE,
WHICH PROVIDES A FUN-FILLED,
INTERACTIVE GALLERY DESIGNED
TO INSPIRE CREATIVITY IN "KIDS"
OF ALL AGES, AND FEATURES AN
ARRAY OF HANDS-ON STATIONS
THAT INTRODUCE VISITORS
TO MASTERPIECES IN THE
PERMANENT COLLECTION.
PHOTO COURTESY OF
CENTER IN THE SQUARE.

3

CHAPTER THREE

CAN YOU COME OUT AND PLAY?

By Dan Smith

THE BEAUTY OF THE VALLEY SURROUNDS THOSE
WHO CHOOSE TO RESIDE IN ROANOKE
OR SIMPLY VISIT FOR A TIME.

PHOTO BY DOUG MILLER.

In the 1970s and 1980s, futurists forecasted that workers in the United States would be drowning in leisure time by the turn of the century and that their most significant challenges would involve how to spend that time. Governments and private entrepreneurs became busy planning to help people take advantage of that wealth of spare time—developing programs, inventing gizmos, and finding uses for high technology.

The infrastructure to maximize use of leisure time was put into place. But something strange happened along the way: Americans began working longer and working harder. Those anticipated leisure hours began to look like a pipe dream.

However, the infrastructure for quality of life activities did not go to waste, especially in Roanoke County, sitting as it does right in the middle of one of the most leisure-friendly plots on earth.

While Roanoke Countians worked harder, they also played harder, played longer, played into their later years, and took up activities not available to large segments of them in earlier decades.

The Roanoke County Department of Parks and Recreation set something of a standard for organizing activities for its citizens of every stripe as the century turned, evolving from a department in charge of children's games to an all-inclusive

THE ROANOKE COUNTY DEPARTMENT OF PARKS AND RECREATION PROVIDES YOUTH SPORTS FOR BOTH GIRLS AND BOYS. THE OPTIONS FOR GIRLS HAVE INCREASED OVER THE RECENT YEARS, AS HAS THE PARTICIPATION OF FEMALES IN SPORTS ACTIVITIES. PHOTOS BY DAN SMITH.

division of government that many consider to be as essential to life as police, fire, and rescue services.

An aging population, bolstered by the huge numbers of post-World War II baby boomers moving through middle age and looking toward retirement, put new types of demands on planners for activities and services. It challenged the creative juices of those in private industry and government to provide services and opportunities to remain active.

The Brambleton Center, ground zero for arts, crafts, life skills programs, and various forms of exercise, dance, and the like, was visited by 70,000 people in 1999, and its growth chart as the century ended was dramatically upward.

In Roanoke County, the Ogden Social Service Organization, founded during World War II, remained active but with a much different focus than rolling bandages. Roanoke County's programs for the elderly, consolidated during the last decade of the twentieth century into the Brambleton Center, are a thriving hotbed of activity. Healthy aging patrons are involved in everything from crafts to dancing to field trips, and an intensely popular bridge night is housed adjacent to a booming teen center. The physical closeness of the distant generations often results in positive vibes and good karma for both.

Roanoke County's citizens are active in sports, as well. There are nearly 300 baseball and softball teams with 3,400 players in 1999; 177 soccer teams with 2,300 players; and 21 football teams with 500 players. Basketball is big, especially with the growth in the participation levels of females, empowered by the 30-year-old federal Title IX law.

The participation of females has been felt dramatically throughout recreation and leisure activities. In fact, softball alone grew from 17 teams in Cave Spring in 1991 to 41 in 1999. The sport expanded from 51 teams countywide in 1991 to 87 in 1998. Girls' basketball participation increased from 140 teams in 1988 to 203 in 1998. Those numbers are being felt at the four public high schools, as well. Female teams have been remarkably successful in basketball, softball, and soccer on a state level.

Aside from senior activities and youth athletics, the government is involved in developing the County in other ways. The Roanoke River Greenway is an example of governmental cooperation in the Roanoke Valley, which is necessary to complete the strip that extends from the Montgomery County line to Explore Park and eventually to Smith Mountain Lake. It is an ambitious project, built in spurts through rural, suburban, and urban vistas, giving walkers, runners, bikers, and skaters safe and beautiful surroundings for their leisure activities.

Still, recreation in Roanoke County isn't simply a matter of the government organizing people. It is growing attractions like the 1840s-era town Explore Park, which recently built a challenging mountain-bicycle trail; the nationally renowned Appalachian Trail; the Blue Ridge Parkway, with its myriad of activities for individuals and groups; and 42 parks. Recreation is hiking or jogging in suburban neighborhoods; exercising at a variety of health clubs and spas; enjoying sports activities at one of several country, golf, tennis, or swim clubs; shooting at archery

IN 1999, ROANOKE CITY AND ROANOKE COUNTY COLLABORATED ON A SKATEBOARD AND ROLLER SKATE PARK IN THE WASENA SECTION OF ROANOKE, AND THE USE OF THE PARK BY YOUNG TEENS IS ASTONISHING. THE PARK PROVIDES A PLACE FOR THESE TEENAGERS TO GATHER ASIDE FROM PARKING LOTS AND SHOPPING MALLS. PHOTO BY DAN SMITH.

and gun ranges; rock climbing on Dragon's Tooth; mud running at Green Hill Park; and celebrating local heritage at Native American pow-wows, Celtic clan gatherings, or music festivals.

In April 2000, ground was broken for the $1.8-million Blue Ridge Parkway Interpretive Center just off the Parkway in Roanoke County. The center will feature exhibits on the construction of the 470-mile roadway and information on attractions in Western Virginia. It is expected to be completed in early 2001.

The County's parks—ranging from the very small neighborhood varieties to the mammoth 220-acre Green Hill Park in Glenvar—are centers of activity. Roanoke County, which has a $3.5-million parks and recreation department budget, 56 full-time employees, and 250 part-timers (ranging from therapists to aerobics instructors and referees), maintains

839 acres of park lands. A new regional park in southwest Roanoke County will have at least 55 acres when completed in the near future.

Roanoke City and Roanoke County collaborated in 1999 on a skateboard and roller skate park in the Wasena section of Roanoke, and the use of the park by young teens is astonishing. These kids, who have been shooed off from every venue where they had tried their sport—mostly busy urban areas and suburban malls—are finally accommodated and have reacted accordingly. Likewise, the teen center at Roanoke County's Brambleton Center is used by youngsters from both Roanoke County and Roanoke City, nearly 30 a day on average and many more for special events.

Hiking and mountain-biking trails are increasingly used. The Appalachian Trail destinations of McAfee's Knob, Tinker Cliffs, and Dragon's Tooth are enormously popular,

but also there are scattered trails along the Blue Ridge Parkway's 17 miles through the Roanoke Valley, and nearby trails feature spectacular vistas, waterfalls, great camping, and hunting. A 15-minute drive from just about anywhere in Roanoke County can still put you into an isolated rural setting with few signs of civilization.

The relatively new Spring Hollow Reservoir has the potential to be used as a recreation center, while its overlook draws a number of visitors. Camp Roanoke is approaching completion near the reservoir and features eight residential cabins, a dining room, and a ropes course in its initial phase.

As Roanoke Countians wrestle with their philosophy of working long hours for the good life, it is becoming increasingly evident that quality of life is sitting here waiting to be enjoyed by anyone who cares to take part. ■

THE POPULARITY OF GOLF HAS
EXPLODED OVER THE PAST FEW
YEARS, AND ITS CHOICE AS A
RECREATIONAL SPORT IN
ROANOKE IS NO DIFFERENT
THAN ANYWHERE ELSE IN
THE COUNTRY. THE ROANOKE
AREA BOASTS AN ARRAY OF
PRIVATE AND PUBLIC COURSES
THROUGHOUT THE COUNTY
AND VALLEY. PHOTO BY
BUDDY WELLS.

ANYONE WISHING TO TRADE IN
THE CONCRETE AND PAVEMENT
FOR HIKING TRAILS AND ROCKY
MOUNTAINS HAS A SHORT
RIDE TO ONE OF MANY PARKS
SITUATED THROUGHOUT THE
REGION. FROM THE COLORFUL
FALL FOLIAGE OF WOODS IN
EXPLORE PARK TO THE BREATH-
TAKING VIEW OF THE VALLEY
FROM DRAGON'S TOOTH ON THE
APPALACHIAN TRAIL, HIKERS
AND CAMPERS CAN FIND
UNMATCHED BEAUTY IN THE
WILDERNESS OF VIRGINIA.
PHOTOS BY DAN SMITH.

4

CHAPTER
FOUR

GETTING TO WORK ON TIME

By Christian Moody

MORE THAN 200,000 PEOPLE MAKE THEIR WAY
TO HOME OR SCHOOL EACH WEEKDAY, BUT MOST
GET TO WORK AND BACK HOME AGAIN WITH
A COMMUTE BEST MEASURED
IN MINUTES, NOT HOURS.

PHOTO BY DOUG MILLER.

Hate traffic? Who doesn't? However, for Roanoke Valley residents, traffic is not the biggest concern of the day. Sure, more than 200,000 people make their way to home or school on a typical weekday, but leaving home hours before sunrise for the express purpose of avoiding gridlock is not a necessary habit among Valley residents. Most get to work and back home again with a commute best measured in minutes, not hours.

To suggest there are no trouble spots with routine traffic problems would be wrong. Some areas cause commuter headaches, no question. But for the most part, the pall of densely populated regions becomes painfully obvious when that next traffic light up ahead cycles from red to green and back to red again without being relegated to a memory in the rearview mirror. Thankfully, such instances are rare in the Roanoke Valley.

The reasons for the absence of massive traffic congestion are varied and, in some cases, apparently unintentional. It's true the daily migration features the majority of commuters driving from the suburbs, mostly in Roanoke County, to the urban center of Roanoke, where the large office buildings are located. But that vector is not always pointing in the same direction. As Roanoke County surrounds Roanoke and Salem, its commuters tend to move inward. But a combination of Interstates 81 and 581, along with U.S. 220 and Virginia 419, effectively form a ring around the urban center, so traffic is just as heavy in each direction of the circumference.

A second factor is the spread location of the Roanoke Valley's largest employers. While Roanoke's central business district is a home base to corporate giant Norfolk Southern and within earshot of its yards and shops, other employers, particularly manufacturing plants, are away from the downtown area.

Roanoke County's turn-of-the-century industrial developments are located in pastoral areas, offering little local traffic to hinder the smooth flow of commerce. R.R. Donnelley built a picturesque book-printing plant in Valley TechPark, a development the County built in a location which took advantage of its proximity to the interstate and distance from downtown. The four companies located in Valley TechPark employ about 600 people.

INDUSTRIAL PARKS, SUCH AS VALLEY POINTE AND VALLEY TECHPARK, HAVE BEEN DEVELOPED THROUGHOUT THE COUNTY IN LOCATIONS THAT TAKE ADVANTAGE OF THEIR PROXIMITY TO THE INTERSTATE AND DOWNTOWN. PHOTO BY DOUG MILLER.

OPTICAL CABLE CORPORATION MANUFACTURES FLAME-RETARDANT FIBER OPTIC CABLES FOR HIGH BANDWIDTH TRANSMISSION OF TELECOMMUNICATIONS. THE OPTICAL FIBER IS PROTECTED UTILIZING A TIGHT-BUFFER COATING PROCESS ALLOWING IT TO BE USED OUTDOORS, AS WELL AS INDOORS, AND OVER MEDIUM DISTANCES. PHOTO BY DOUG MILLER

Near Valley TechPark, on the site of a former farm and adjacent to I-81, the County has planned the Center for Research Technology (CRT) development, a unique high-tech business park which will feature a combination of large and small companies located on a physically beautiful piece of land. CRT will take advantage of the scenic vistas, the hilly terrain, and the farm ponds at the site to provide a special setting for the businesses and their employees.

Virginia 419, itself, is a corridor of business, almost by accident. Three of the largest employers are within two miles of each other along 419—GE Drive Systems employs about 1,550, primarily engineers, managers, and manufacturing laborers; Yokohama Tire Corporation is a labor-intensive plant employing over 1,000; and Lewis-Gale Hospital employs 2,300.

Virginia 419 has become an office park pipeline through the County. Ironically, the original planners never thought of the road as anything other than a bypass, a quicker way to get from the southern part of the Valley to the western portion. Businesses saw the benefit of locating on the transportation corridor.

Roanoke was built on the rails of Norfolk & Western Railway in the 1880s. The railroad changed the sleepy little town of Big Lick, hovering near Salem, which did not want the railroad headquarters, into an industrial and transportation center. That heritage is deeply entrenched.

Yet somewhere along the line, the Roanoke Valley became a health care hub. Norfolk Southern, as the railway is now named, employs nearly 3,000 people, but that pales in comparison to the 7,100 of Carilion Health System

ABOVE: ITT HAS MADE THE DIFFICULT TRANSITION FROM A BUSINESS HEAVILY DEPENDENT ON MILITARY CONTRACTS IN THE EARLY 1990S TO A MANUFACTURER FOR THE PRIVATE SECTOR WITH ITS NIGHTVISION GOGGLES. PHOTO BY DOUG MILLER. LEFT: ALTHOUGH THE ROANOKE ECONOMY IS STILL BASED LARGELY ON MANUFACTURING AND INDUSTRY, THE INTRODUCTION OF MODERN TECHNOLOGY HAS VASTLY IMPROVED THE EFFICIENCY OF THESE COMPANIES, AS WELL AS THE QUALITY OF THEIR PRODUCTS. PHOTO BY DOUG MILLER.

R.R. DONNELLEY COMPANY RECENTLY OPENED A PRINTING PLANT IN VALLEY TECHPARK. THE COMPANY OFFERS COMMERCIAL PRINTING AND INFORMATION SERVICES IN A NUMBER OF MARKETS TO VARIED MEDIA. EMPLOYEES AT R.R. DONNELLEY ARE DEDICATED TO PRODUCING QUALITY PRODUCTS FOR THEIR CLIENTS. PHOTOS BY DOUG MILLER.

(which includes Roanoke Memorial and Community Hospitals and a number of satellite services), the Valley's largest private employer.

Combining Carilion's numbers with the 2,300 employed by Lewis-Gale, a Columbia HCA company, and the 1,600 who work for the federal government at the Veterans Affairs Hospital in Salem, more than 11,000 people work in the health care field in the Roanoke Valley.

While any population center needs manufacturing jobs, the current focus is on environmentally friendly alternatives. Old economy companies in banking and insurance find the Valley accommodating. First Union National Bank kept an operations center in the County after acquiring Dominion Bankshares, a bank headquartered in Roanoke. That center, along with the First Union branches, employs nearly 2,000. Bank office centers, in fact, form something of a backbone of employment at the lower levels.

ITT Defense is an example of the type of industry economic developers are targeting. The company employs engineers, administrators, and manufacturing personnel for specialized products. Employing about 900 in 2000, ITT Defense is among the sector of businesses which developers want to bring to the Valley. ITT has made the difficult transition from a business heavily dependent on military contracts in the early 1990s to a manufacturer for the private sector with its nightvision goggles.

Electronics and hardware, from resistors to robotics, are the business ideas sought in an effort to increase the level of employment within the Valley. Transportation systems and equipment is also a targeted industry, along with biotechnology and biomedical equipment, an industry sure to expand exponentially with the new Carilion Biomedical Institute, a major medical research facility in which Virginia Tech and the University of Virginia are partners, operating at full bore. Since those two industries have such a strong presence already, adding the supplying firms is a logical progression.

Unemployment is historically low in the Valley. It is so low, in fact, that economic developers prefer a statistic on underemployment—individuals working in jobs requiring fewer skills and paying less than positions for which they have training and education. The addition of companies offering high-paying, low-impact, environmentally friendly jobs will continue to be a goal throughout the Roanoke Valley, as it is elsewhere in the country.

Still, retail and service jobs are being added frequently. While construction companies are working toward building new industrial locations, the shopping centers are keeping pace. The Roanoke Valley now has more places to spend money than ever before, and that trend will only increase.

Education at all levels is an industry in the Valley where thousands of people make an impact. The school systems themselves employ more than 3,600 people. That does not take into account private schools, preschools, or other avenues of education. Two four-year colleges, Virginia Western Community College, various college satellite programs, and several trade schools within the Valley indicate that there are thousands of people willing to educate the masses.

More and more, manufacturing and service jobs are joining health care as being 24-hour operations. Grocery and discount stores are open around the clock. Trucks leave warehouses at all hours, taking advantage of one of the most heavily traveled roads in the United States, I-81. And, as always, doctors and nurses care for patients, firefighters battle blazes, and police protect the community no matter what time of day or night it might be.

Of course, diversifying business hours so all employees aren't on the road at the same time is an important factor in alleviating traffic problems. Whatever the cause, not many are complaining. ∎

TRUCKS LEAVE WAREHOUSES AT ALL HOURS, TAKING ADVANTAGE OF ONE OF THE MOST HEAVILY TRAVELED ROADS IN THE UNITED STATES, I-81. KROGER IS ONE SUCH COMPANY WHICH RELIES ON DIESEL TRUCKS TO DISTRIBUTE FOOD, PHARMACY MERCHANDISE, AND OTHER PRODUCTS NATIONWIDE. PHOTOS BY DOUG MILLER.

FROM INSURANCE COMPANIES
TO MANUFACTURERS,
BUSINESSES IN THE ROANOKE
AREA UTILIZE THE LATEST IN
TECHNOLOGY TO OFFER THE BEST
SERVICE TO THEIR CUSTOMERS,
WHILE ALSO BEING ABLE TO
ACCURATELY MAINTAIN DATA
AND QUICKLY ACCESS THE
INTERNET. PHOTOS BY
DOUG MILLER.

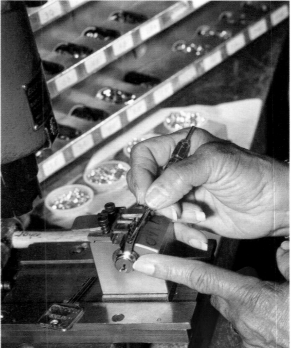

ELECTRONICS AND HARDWARE, FROM RESISTORS TO ROBOTICS, ARE THE BUSINESS IDEAS SOUGHT IN AN EFFORT TO INCREASE THE LEVEL OF EMPLOYMENT WITHIN THE VALLEY. PHOTOS BY DOUG MILLER.

ABOVE: THOUGH THE NEED FOR STEEL HAS CHANGED WITH THE PROGRESSION OF TECHNOLOGY, IT REMAINS AN IMPORTANT COMPONENT FROM COMMERCIAL PRODUCTS SUCH AS SLABS AND BEAMS TO SMALLER ITEMS INCLUDING FIRE EXTINGUISHERS. PHOTOS BY DAN SMITH.
RIGHT: A MAJOR UNITED PARCEL SERVICE HUB SITS NEARLY ADJACENT TO THE AIRPORT AND SERVES WESTERN VIRGINIA BY TRANSPORTING A LARGE QUANTITY OF THE MORE THAN 2,000 TONS OF FREIGHT AND CARGO SHIPPED THROUGH THE AIRPORT EACH MONTH. PHOTO BY DAN SMITH.

LEFT: ONE OF THE THREE LARGEST AREA EMPLOYERS, GE DRIVE SYSTEMS EMPLOYS ABOUT 1,550, PRIMARILY ENGINEERS, MANAGERS, AND MANUFACTURING LABORERS. PHOTO BY DAN SMITH.

ABOVE: RETAIL AND SERVICE JOBS ARE BEING ADDED FREQUENTLY, AND, THEREFORE, CONSTRUCTION COMPANIES ARE WORKING TOWARD BUILDING NEW INDUSTRIAL LOCATIONS. PHOTOS BY DAN SMITH.

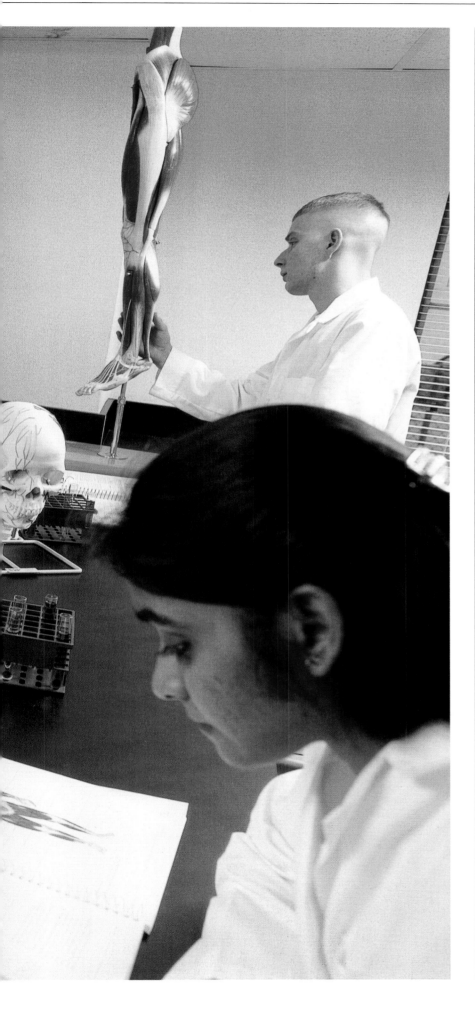

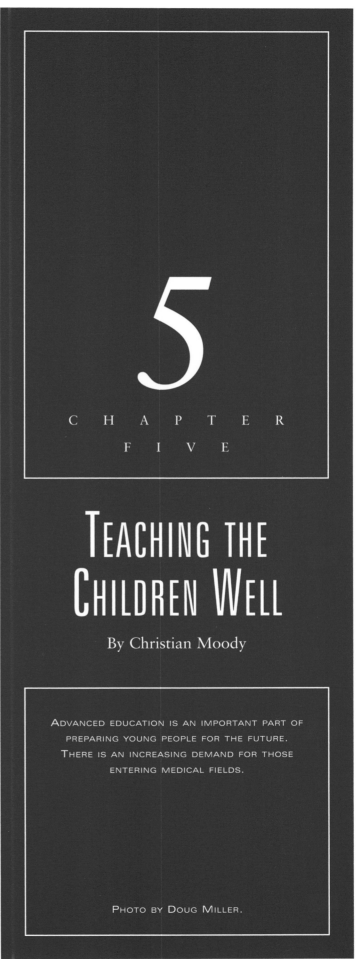

5

C H A P T E R
F I V E

TEACHING THE CHILDREN WELL

By Christian Moody

ADVANCED EDUCATION IS AN IMPORTANT PART OF
PREPARING YOUNG PEOPLE FOR THE FUTURE.
THERE IS AN INCREASING DEMAND FOR THOSE
ENTERING MEDICAL FIELDS.

PHOTO BY DOUG MILLER.

ELEMENTARY EDUCATION IN
ROANOKE IS A DIVERSE
COMBINATION OF PLAYTIME,
IN-CLASS LEARNING, AND OTHER
PROGRAMS, WHICH NOT ONLY
TEACH THE CHILDREN, BUT
PROVIDE THEM WITH LIFE SKILLS
SUCH AS SELF-CONFIDENCE.
SPECIAL EDUCATION IS ALSO
A TOP PRIORITY FOR THE
EDUCATIONAL SYSTEM.
STUDENTS AT ALL LEVELS ARE
GIVEN THE SAME OPPORTUNITIES
TO LEARN. PHOTOS BY
DOUG MILLER.

It is no secret that education is a major priority in Roanoke County. As the area's largest school system, the school division receives widespread recognition for academic excellence and ranks among the state's top school systems with both verbal and math achievements exceeding the state and national averages. The division is also credited with having the largest dual-enrollment/college-credit program in Southwest and Central Virginia. Roanoke County Schools are dedicated to providing lifelong learning through a multitude of educational opportunities in an effort to synchronize the latest technology with traditional courses of study. This exceptional instruction educates more than 14,000 children from kindergarten through 12th grade annually. Success within the school district is further evidenced through 90.2 percent of the division's eighth-grade students passing the Standards of Learning (SOL) technology test. Back Creek Elementary and Cave Spring Elementary Schools were two of the 6.5 percent of Virginia schools which achieved a 70-percent pass rate in all subjects and were fully accredited by the State Board of Education.

Because 80 percent of all jobs today require technical training, skill precision is taught at the Arnold R. Burton Technology Center. Through the classes offered at this facility, students participate in high intensity technology programs, combined with the required academic courses. The center strives to further students' knowledge through hands-on learning centered on such topics as graphic design, electricity, electronics, power mechanics and welding, auto service technology, masonry, carpentry, child care, cosmetology, health assistance, landscaping, industrial training, and manufacturing processes. Many of the career and technical education classes, as well as advanced English, history, and government classes, give college credit from Virginia Western Community College or advanced placement credit. The classes enable students to graduate from Roanoke County Schools with several hours of college credit if they choose.

Roanoke County has joined with six other area school divisions to offer instruction at the Roanoke Valley Governor's School. This special regional public school offers a curriculum focused on science, mathematics, and technology.

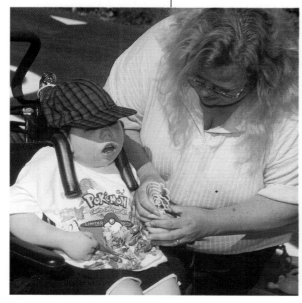

EDUCATION IS A MAJOR
PRIORITY IN THE REGION, AND
ONE OF THE SERVICES PROVIDED
BY ROANOKE COUNTY IS
TRANSPORTATION TO SCHOOL
FOR ITS CHILDREN. PHOTO BY
DAN SMITH.

The school has served as a model institution for other facilities throughout the state and the nation.

Roanoke County is also the state's second-largest adult education provider, serving more than 10,000 people annually with adult courses and diverse program offerings, ranging from evening high school classes to programs structured for senior citizens. As a business-focused in-house training program, numerous computer classes are offered for personal use, preparation for employment, further training for advancement, and preparation for new careers. Classes focus on marketing, trade and industry, and professional development.

To ensure an educated future, the Roanoke County School Division strives to prepare its students to blend rigorous academic courses with technical/vocational classes and interpersonal skills. This effort attempts to maximize each individual's full potential to achieve true excellence in education.

In addition to the 28 public schools in the County, quality education also is available through private and independent instruction offered in schools such as North Cross, Roanoke Catholic, Community, and Roanoke Valley Christian.

Roanoke County residents have access to a myriad of higher educational opportunities, as well. Rich in history, Roanoke College was founded in Salem in 1847. It remains the nation's second oldest and Virginia's only Lutheran college. The school has received national recognition as one of the premier liberal arts colleges in the United States.

Hollins University, Virginia's first chartered women's college, has received national acclaim in the *New York Times, Washington Post, Southern Living,* and *Esquire* for the work of its graduates and its distinctive approach to teaching. The school offers a challenging liberal arts program with 30 majors, and established a coed graduate program in 1958. Hollins' creative writing program has launched some of the most powerful voices in contemporary fiction.

Situated on a 70-acre campus located in southwest Roanoke, Virginia Western Community College is a two-year institution of higher education, operating under a 23-school statewide system of community colleges. The school offers day, evening, and weekend classes to a six-county region and awards associate degrees in a variety of technical and academic areas.

Helping to address the needs of the business community, National Business College, the Dominion Business School, Bluefield College, the Electronic Computer Programming Institute, and Averett College operate programs in the Valley, offering specialized degrees in a variety of occupational fields. Specializing in health care, the College of Health Sciences offers baccalaureate and associate degrees in such areas as physician assistance, occupational therapy, and nursing. The educational opportunities available through the college, which include practical experience at Carilion Health Systems, one of the commonwealth's largest private health facilities, enable students to earn a degree while learning a specific skill to apply in the world of work.

To further expand the educational opportunities offered to the residents of Southwest Virginia, five colleges and universities are represented within the Roanoke Valley Graduate Center. This cooperative effort offers quality graduate and professional development programs to part-time adult students primarily during the evenings and weekends, though some weekday programs also are offered through the school. Courses are taught by professors on-site, as well as through advanced interactive electronic delivery. Southwest Virginia is also home to two state-supported universities, Radford and Virginia Tech, both located a short drive from the Roanoke Valley.

Education in the Roanoke Valley is taken seriously, and workforce development is an important concern to the school systems, the governments, and the business community. With the variety of opportunity available to Roanoke Valley residents, there is something for everyone. ■

HIGH SCHOOL STUDENTS
RECEIVE THE SAME EDUCATIONAL
ADVANTAGES AS DO THE
ELEMENTARY CHILDREN,
THROUGH SPECIAL EDUCATION
CLASSES OR SCIENCE AND
COMPUTER LABORATORIES.
PHOTOS BY DOUG MILLER.

HIGH SCHOOL GRADUATES HAVE SEVERAL OPTIONS TO FURTHER OR COMPLETE THEIR EDUCATION, FROM TECHNICAL SCHOOLS, WHICH TEACH THE NEWEST TECHNOLOGY, TO COMMUNITY COLLEGES AND LOCAL UNIVERSITIES, WHICH OFFER STANDARD AND SPECIALIZED COURSES. PHOTOS BY DOUG MILLER.

ROANOKE COLLEGE, THE SECOND OLDEST LUTHERAN-RELATED COLLEGE IN AMERICA, IS A FOUR-YEAR LIBERAL ARTS SCHOOL SITUATED IN SALEM. THE COLLEGE HAS BEEN RANKED AMONG *U.S. NEWS & WORLD REPORT*'S TOP 10 REGIONAL LIBERAL ARTS COLLEGES IN THE SOUTH FOR SIX CONSECUTIVE YEARS. FOUNDED IN 1842, MANY OF THE ORIGINAL BUILDINGS STILL SERVE THE STUDENTS WELL. PHOTO BY DAN SMITH.

HOLLINS UNIVERSITY WAS FOUNDED IN THE SAME YEAR AS ROANOKE COLLEGE, BUT THE SCHOOL WAS THE FIRST CHARTERED WOMAN'S COLLEGE IN VIRGINIA. THEN, IN 1958, HOLLINS ESTABLISHED COED GRADUATE PROGRAMS. HOLLINS HAS BEEN RANKED BY SEVERAL NATIONAL PUBLICATIONS AS ONE OF THE BEST EDUCATIONAL INVESTMENTS IN AMERICA FOR NOT ONLY ITS ACADEMIC AND LIBERAL ARTS PROGRAMS, BUT ALSO FOR ITS QUALITY OF LIFE AND COST OF EDUCATION. PHOTO BY TOMMY FIREBAUGH.

THE BEAUTIFUL CAMPUS OF
HOLLINS UNIVERSITY, WHICH
CHANGED ITS NAME IN 1998
FROM HOLLINS COLLEGE, IS
LOCATED IN ROANOKE JUST
MINUTES FROM THE BLUE RIDGE
MOUNTAINS. PHOTO BY
DAN SMITH.

6

CHAPTER SIX

GETTING AROUND

By Christina Koomen Smith

FOR MORE THAN A CENTURY, THE RAILROAD HAS BEEN THE COMMERCIAL LIFELINE OF THE VALLEY, PROVIDING BOTH JOBS AND BUSINESS DEVELOPMENT OPPORTUNITIES. THE NORFOLK SOUTHERN CORPORATION MAINTAINS ONE OF ITS TWO REGIONAL HEADQUARTERS IN DOWNTOWN ROANOKE AND IS A MAJOR EMPLOYER IN THE REGION.

PHOTO BY DAN SMITH.

The Roanoke Valley is the most significant cultural, commercial, and population center in southwest Virginia, and, as such, it is also a major transportation center. Between interstate highways, a busy regional airport, major trucking terminals, and a rail junction that predates Grover Cleveland's administration, all roads, it seems, do, indeed, lead to the Roanoke Valley.

Though Roanoke County was well-entrenched when a major railroad established its headquarters in what was then Big Lick in the late nineteenth century, the valley is still recognized as an area developed—if not built—by the railroad.

When the decision was made to connect the Shenandoah Valley and Norfolk & Western Railways at this quiet crossroads, the newly chartered Town of Roanoke (Big Lick's evolution) began to take off. As the town grew into a city, Roanoke County was ultimately transformed from an agricultural area into a suburban and industrial locality, with transportation growing increasingly important for commercial and cultural activities.

For more than a century, the railroad has been the commercial lifeline of the region, providing both jobs and business development opportunities. Although Norfolk & Western moved its main base of operations to Norfolk, Virginia, following its 1982 merger with Southern Railway, the resulting Norfolk Southern Corporation maintains one of its two regional headquarters in downtown Roanoke and remains a major employer. The company expanded again in the late 1990s, when it entered into a joint agreement with CSX Corporation to acquire Conrail. Norfolk Southern's rail system now comprised 21,800 miles of track in 22 states as the century turned.

Norfolk & Western officially stopped transporting passengers in the 1970s when Amtrak entered the picture (train travelers can make an Amtrak connection at nearby Clifton Forge and Lynchburg), but the company already had a strong freight operation which continues today. The nostalgia for passenger transportation—as well as the reality of crowded interstates and skies—led to a movement in 1998 toward reestablishing passenger traffic. That movement is gaining steam at the beginning of a new century.

More than 100 trains a day carry such commodities as coal, grain, lumber, automobile parts, and military equipment through Norfolk Southern's Roanoke terminal. Much of the behind-the-scenes work of running a major rail system takes place in the Roanoke Valley, too. The Shaffers Crossing Shops maintain and repair an average of 30 locomotives a day, while the Roanoke Shops perform major engine overhauls and serve as a primary railcar building facility. The company also operates a material yard for track components; a solid waste transport service for the Roanoke Valley Resource Authority (the Waste Line Express, which hauls the valley's garbage to the landfill); and a distribution center that handles lumber, paper, and bulk plastic for nonrail customers.

NORFOLK & WESTERN, WHICH MERGED WITH SOUTHERN RAILWAY IN 1982 TO FORM THE NORFOLK SOUTHERN CORPORATION, OFFICIALLY STOPPED TRANSPORTING PASSENGERS IN THE 1970S WHEN AMTRAK ENTERED THE PICTURE, BUT THE COMPANY ALREADY HAD A STRONG FREIGHT OPERATION THAT CONTINUES TODAY. MORE THAN 100 TRAINS A DAY CARRY SUCH COMMODITIES AS COAL, GRAIN, LUMBER, AUTOMOBILE PARTS, AND MILITARY EQUIPMENT THROUGH NORFOLK SOUTHERN'S ROANOKE TERMINAL. PHOTOS BY DAN SMITH.

Compared with trains, air travel is a relative upstart, but aviation in Roanoke County has come a long way since a little Wright Brothers-style plane landed on the grounds of what is now Victory Stadium in 1914. The first actual air service to the region began in 1933, when the Ludington Airlines of Virginia launched a New York to Nashville route which included a stop at the 320-acre Cannaday Farm landing area near the County's northern rim. The following year, American Airlines brought the first shipment of airmail to Roanoke County, an event that attracted 1,500 spectators. But when the Postal Service later canceled its Roanoke run due to the crude conditions at the fledgling airport, aviation supporters knew something had to be done.

In 1937, Roanoke established an Airport Department to oversee future operations at the Roanoke County facility (even though it would be 40 more years before annexation brought the airport within the city limits). Dedicated as Woodrum Field, in honor of airport booster and Sixth District Congressman Clifton A. Woodrum, in 1941, the airport underwent decades of improvements, from immediate and extensive upgrades to its runways to the construction and expansion of a more modern terminal in the late 1980s. In 1967, Piedmont Airlines, the Valley's primary passenger carrier, introduced jet service to the region. As business grew, Woodrum Field was renamed Roanoke Regional Airport, and ownership was subsequently granted to a new regional Airport Commission.

Total enplanements and deplanements have consistently topped 50,000 per month through the 1990s and into 2000. More than 50 percent of the airport's passengers are traveling on business, and major corporate customers include General Electric, First Union, Carilion Health Care, Advance Auto, Allstate, and Hayes, Seay, Mattern & Mattern. The airport also transports more than 2,000 tons of freight and cargo in an average month, as well as around 100 tons of airmail. A major United Parcel Service hub sits nearly adjacent to the airport and serves Western Virginia.

SCENIC RURAL ROADS CONNECT
THE CITIES THAT ENCOMPASS
ROANOKE COUNTY AND VALLEY.
FROM MAGNIFICENT VIEWS OF
SURROUNDING MOUNTAINS
TO SERENE PASTURES OF
COMPLACENT COWS, DRIVERS
CAN ENJOY A PEACEFUL
COMMUTE TO WORK OR RIDE
THROUGH THE COUNTRYSIDE.
PHOTOS BY DOUG MILLER.

agreed that widening I-81 through the Valley is a priority, though no timetable for the project has been set. The I-581 corridor that funnels I-81 traffic towards the city tops them all—at 80,000 vehicles a day, it is the most heavily traveled piece of pavement west of Richmond.

The most significant highway project in Roanoke County at the turn of the century is the proposed Interstate 73, a north-south corridor which will ultimately extend from Detroit to the coast of South Carolina. In Virginia, I-73 is regarded as a valuable link between the Roanoke Valley and North Carolina's Piedmont Triad. Several possible routes for the new road have been identified, and environmental impact studies, citizen forums, and cost and feasibility studies are underway. VDOT held public hearings on the project in the fall of 2000, with the goal of finalizing plans for the new interstate in early 2001.

County planners understand that cars, at least for now, are a necessity for Roanoke County residents. But beyond making maximum and efficient use of existing roads, the County's Community Plan includes strategies for reducing the dependence on automobiles. The County is looking to build sidewalks, walking trails, and bike paths to enable residents to travel safely between residential, commercial, and public spaces without hopping in the car. The Roanoke Valley Greenway—which will extend from the Montgomery County line to Smith Mountain Lake—has already seen significant construction in Roanoke County in 2000, and much more is planned in the coming few years.

The Valley would like to develop its own public transportation resources, including an intermodal air, highway, and rail hub (with truck containers often being carried by train through specific stretches of the region) and even high-speed passenger rail service with destinations like Richmond and Washington, D.C.

Above all, the County places a premium on balancing its transportation needs with its commitment to preserving the local environment. ■

Today, Roanoke Regional Airport serves a 19-county area with four major carriers—US Airways, United Express, Delta Connection, and NW Airlink—offering connections to dozens of domestic and international destinations. Travelers are welcomed by a bright, airy, architecturally interesting, easy-to-navigate terminal complete with such modern amenities as data ports and ATM machines. Visitors often comment about the astonishing setting, and officials appreciate the first impression visitors are given of the Roanoke Valley.

Given our persistently automobile-oriented culture, it is perhaps not surprising that the main mode of transportation in Roanoke County at the turn of the century is cars—more cars, bigger cars, better cars. About 700 miles of primary, secondary, and rural roadways crisscross County land, including portions of Interstate 81 (the second most heavily traveled highway in the Eastern United States), and U.S. Highways 220, 221, 460, and 11. But, despite its reliance on automobiles, Roanoke County has yet to experience the kind of congestion that drives some people to leave more vehicle-clogged areas like northern Virginia and Tidewater.

This is not to say that Roanoke County doesn't have its share of traffic. Route 220 carries some 25,000 vehicles a day on average, while Route 460 carries between 20,000 vehicles a day west of Salem to upwards of 28,000 east of the city. Interstate 81 carries as many as 60,000 vehicles a day through the Roanoke Valley, and anyone who has driven it in recent years will not be at all surprised to learn that up to 40 percent of that traffic is tractor-trailers.

In the late 1990s, a spate of accidents throughout the Roanoke Valley on I-81 led officials to consider the widening of the road and other alternatives to help alleviate the danger. The Virginia Department of Transportation (VDOT) has

ABOUT 700 MILES OF
PRIMARY, SECONDARY, AND
RURAL ROADWAYS CRISSCROSS
COUNTY LAND, INCLUDING
PORTIONS OF INTERSTATE 81
(THE SECOND MOST HEAVILY
TRAVELED HIGHWAY IN THE
EASTERN UNITED STATES), AND
U.S. HIGHWAYS 220, 221,
460, AND 11. THOUGH NOT AS
CONGESTED AS MANY LARGE
CITIES, THE AMOUNT OF TRAFFIC
HAS CREATED THE NEED TO
WIDEN I-81, AS WELL AS
PROPOSE A NEW LINK THROUGH
VIRGINIA, INTERSTATE 73.
PHOTO AT RIGHT BY DAN
SMITH. PHOTO BELOW BY
DOUG MILLER.

ROANOKE'S BUS SYSTEM, VALLEY METRO, IS AN ALTERNATIVE MODE OF TRANSPORTATION TO THOSE NEEDING TO COMMUTE TO WORK OR SHOP, AND THE ROUTES ALLOW PEOPLE TO ACCESS AREA HOSPITALS, AS WELL. PHOTO BY DAN SMITH.

TODAY, ROANOKE REGIONAL AIRPORT SERVES A 19-COUNTY AREA WITH FOUR MAJOR CARRIERS—US AIRWAYS, UNITED EXPRESS, DELTA CONNECTION, AND NW AIRLINK—OFFERING CONNECTIONS TO DOZENS OF DOMESTIC AND INTERNATIONAL DESTINATIONS. TRAVELERS ARE WELCOMED BY A BRIGHT, AIRY, ARCHITECTURALLY INTERESTING, EASY-TO-NAVIGATE MODERN TERMINAL. PHOTO BY TOMMY FIREBAUGH.

OUTLYING COMMUNITIES SUCH
AS CATAWBA VALLEY, BENT
MOUNTAIN, AND WINDY GAP
PROVIDE THE PERFECT BACKDROP
FOR PEACEFUL DRIVES THROUGH
THE QUIET COUNTRYSIDE. PHOTO
BY DOUG MILLER.

7

C H A P T E R
S E V E N

IF YOU HAVE
TO ASK...

By Christina Koomen Smith

RESIDENTS OF ROANOKE CAN CHOSE TO LIVE IN
THE COZINESS OF QUAINT CITY NEIGHBORHOODS
OR ON TOP OF A MOUNTAIN AMID THE
BLOSSOMING TREES AND SCENIC COUNTRYSIDE.

PHOTO BY DOUG MILLER.

Ask what creates the kind of place where people love to be, and you're likely to hear "quality of life" somewhere in the response. Popular as a catch phrase used by government and civic organizations to encourage economic development, the concept of "quality of life" includes a constellation of characteristics which make a place truly livable. And yet, ask anyone to describe those characteristics and you could easily get a blank stare. In fact, the less folks have to think about the ingredients, the better off they probably are.

Perhaps the first thing that comes to mind is environment, and with its ubiquitous mountain scenery, Roanoke County

is off to a good start. Situated in the valley between the Appalachian and Blue Ridge Mountains, Roanoke County enjoys a full tableau of seasonal change, from the splash of redbud and forsythia blooming in the spring to a brilliant palette of colorful Eastern hardwood foliage in the fall.

The climate is generally mild even in the summer and winter months, with average temperatures ranging from a July high of 86 to a January low of 25. The Roanoke Valley area averages about 100 bright, clear days a year, and extreme weather events are rare. Blessed with green open spaces, and traversed by the Roanoke River and its tributaries, the County is also graced by the tidy skyline and bustling market square of the City of Roanoke, as well as the charming and historic streets of Salem.

Economic vitality is an important consideration for most residents, and Roanoke County at the turn of the century has an impressive resume. Part of a region which *Inc.* magazine, in the late 1990s, called one of the top 100 places in the nation for business development, the County outperforms the state, and even the nation, on a variety of measures.

The Roanoke Valley's cost of living index at the beginning of the century is 96.8 overall (as compared with the national benchmark of 100), surpassing Norfolk (97.7) and Richmond (108.3) in Virginia, as well as such metro areas as Raleigh (101.8) and San Diego (127.8). The Roanoke Valley exceeds the national average in every individual category, as well. Those were transportation, housing, utilities, health care, grocery items, and miscellaneous goods and services.

According to the figures, Roanoke County in 2000 has one of the highest household incomes in the region, with 32 percent of its families bringing home over $50,000 per year (compared with 28 percent statewide). What's more, growth in family income outpaced growth in the consumer price index in recent years, which has meant increasing affluence for County residents.

QUALITY HEALTH CARE IS IMPORTANT TO THE CITIZENS OF ROANOKE, AND THE AREA IS SERVED BY SEVERAL HOSPITALS AND CLINICS, AS WELL AS A VETERAN'S HOSPITAL. THE REGION OFFERS LOW-COST, QUALITY HEALTH CARE, AND ROANOKE HAS BEEN CITED AS ONE OF THE 10 HEALTHIEST PLACES IN THE U.S. TO LIVE BY *KIPLINGER'S PERSONAL FINANCE MAGAZINE*. PHOTO BY DAN SMITH. RIGHT: LOCATED IN SALEM, THE LEWIS-GALE MEDICAL CENTER ENCOMPASSES BOTH A FULL-SERVICE HOSPITAL AND A TREATMENT CLINIC. PHOTO BY DAN SMITH.

CARILION'S ROANOKE
MEMORIAL AND COMMUNITY
HOSPITALS OFFER
COMPREHENSIVE HEALTH CARE,
FROM EMERGENCY AND TRAUMA
SERVICES TO INPATIENT CARE,
SURGERY, REHABILITATION,
AND BEHAVIORAL MEDICINE.
CARILION ALSO RUNS THE
LONG-ESTABLISHED CANCER
CENTER OF WESTERN VIRGINIA.
PHOTOS BY DAN SMITH.

Another of Roanoke County's advantages is the affordability of housing. Valley-wide, the median price of a home is $110,000, significantly less than the state median of $125,000. Statistics show that the County's housing inventory was 74 percent owner-occupied, 22 percent renter-occupied, and only four percent vacant for the past two decades of the twentieth century, indicating a healthy and stable real estate market.

Roanoke County's new cluster housing ordinance, intended to protect and expand green spaces in future developments, is being met with open arms by both residents of Roanoke County and developers. The plan, the first of its kind in the region, is designed with more flexibility for builders in mind. They are able to design neighborhoods that lend themselves to the preservation of woodlands, green space, and mountain slopes.

The new ordinance has freed developers from minimum lot size requirements and allows them to build private roads whose standards are not as rigid as for public roads. Cluster housing allows six single-family homes per acre with limited setback requirements. The ordinance replaces one allowing two or three houses per acre. With the regulations, builders are required to preserve 35 to 50 percent of land as open space.

Like the real estate market, Roanoke County's employment picture is robust. The Virginia Employment Commission's most up-to-the-minute unemployment rate for Roanoke County was 1.1 percent early in 2000, one of the lowest rates among all counties and cities in the state. Several of the region's largest employers are in the County, and residents report that one of the things they appreciate most is having an easy commute to the workplace, wherever it happens to be.

Roanoke Valley is one of the 10 best places in the country to raise a family according to *Inc.* magazine, partly because Roanoke County residents enjoy an abundance of services, as well as myriad cultural and recreational opportunities.

Parents of school-age children are well aware that the Roanoke County public school system has consistently had one of the best report cards around (in fact, the U.S. Department of Education has recognized the Roanoke Valley's schools for being among the best in the country). Comprised of 17 elementary schools, two middle schools, three junior high schools, and five high schools, the County system served approximately 13,800 pupils in 2000. Student-to-teacher ratios ranged from 21 to 1 at the elementary level to 23 to 1 in high school. The high schools' 98 percent graduation rate included 80 percent who went on to some form of post-secondary education. To accommodate a growing population, a new high school is planned to open in the southern part of the County in the fall of 2002. In addition, there are three private schools in the County serving children from preschool through 12th grades.

Families are safe in Roanoke County, where in 1998 there was only one homicide, compared with nearly 30 in the suburban counties around Richmond. The overall crime rate was less than two-thirds of the state's average, and less than half the national average. In fact, recent statistics indicate that the incidence of crime in Roanoke County was even less than that reported in some of the state's more rural counties.

County residents have easy access to several major hospitals. Carilion's Roanoke Memorial and Community Hospitals, in the City of Roanoke, offer comprehensive health care, from emergency and trauma services to inpatient care, surgery, rehabilitation, and behavioral medicine. Carilion also runs the long-established Cancer Center of Western Virginia.

In Salem, the Lewis-Gale Medical Center and the Veterans Administration Medical Center offer a full range of hospitalization, emergency treatment, and clinic-based health services. Tucked away in the western mountains, the old Catawba sanitarium that housed tuberculosis patients in the early twentieth century has become an accredited hospital in its own right, serving primarily the mental health needs of geriatric patients.

Following the national trend of providing better lifestyle options for seniors, Roanoke County has a number of retirement villages and long-term care facilities to choose from. This is a treatment and care area that is growing exponentially as the baby boomers near retirement age, caring first for their parents, and eventually for themselves.

Beyond the basic necessities, however, quality of life also means enjoyment, and with three distinct metro areas within its borders, Roanoke County does not lack for cultural or recreational opportunities.

ABOVE: THE NEWEST TECHNOLOGY IS UTILIZED BY HEALTH CARE FACILITIES THROUGHOUT THE REGION IN TREATING PATIENTS WITH CANCER AND OTHER CHRONIC ILLNESSES. PHOTO BY DOUG MILLER.

RIGHT AND OPPOSITE: THE VETERANS ADMINISTRATION MEDICAL CENTER OFFERS A FULL RANGE OF HOSPITALIZATION, EMERGENCY TREATMENT, AND CLINIC-BASED HEALTH SERVICES THROUGH BOTH THE HOSPITAL AND CLINIC IN SALEM. PHOTOS BY DAN SMITH.

Two civic centers—one in Roanoke, one in Salem—offer year-round entertainment, from music and dance to home shows, horse shows, and more. Roanoke College in Salem and Hollins University in North County present a variety of interesting speakers, performances, and symposia that are open to the public, and they offer many educational opportunities for people in the community.

The greater Roanoke area boasts baseball, ice hockey, and soccer teams, and in the spring of 2000, added arena football to its lineup of professional sports. County residents can enjoy such diverse attractions as downtown Roanoke's Center in the Square, the Mill Mountain Zoo, Dixie Caverns, and the pioneer history Explore Park, just off the Blue Ridge Parkway. From museums to theater to restaurants to shopping centers to a full calendar of festivals and other events, there's something for everyone in Roanoke County.

The more people discover Roanoke County, the more important it becomes to protect the quality of life, so cherished by residents and visitors alike. The County is growing at a relatively measured pace (less than one percent per year), compared with some of its suburban counterparts.

While there is a need for a strong economic base to support a growing population, the County government is taking an active approach to preserving the many features which make the County thoroughly livable. The 1998 Community Plan outlines a variety of strategies for achieving this goal, such as encouraging high-tech, nonindustrial business development, creating neighborhood design guidelines, supporting cultural and recreational organizations, and expanding the parks and greenways system.

As they go about their daily routines, residents might not think much about quality of life, about what it means or how Roanoke County measures up. It's a matter of knowing it when you see it. Ask anyone to define quality of life and you probably won't be sent to the statistics and the record books. You'll probably be told to look around you. ■

NEWER RESIDENTIAL HOUSING
BEING BUILT IN OUTLYING AREAS
SUCH AS IN CAVE SPRING AND
HUNTING HILLS PROVIDE
ALL THE NECESSITIES OF A
NEIGHBORHOOD AND THE
PEACEFULNESS OF SUBURBAN
LIFE. PHOTOS BY DOUG MILLER.

ABOVE: HISTORIC VICTORIAN HOMES LINE THE QUIET STREETS OF SALEM, WHERE RESIDENTS CAN ENJOY THE CLOSENESS OF NEIGHBORS AND THE AMENITIES OF A SMALL TOWN. PHOTO BY DAN SMITH.
RIGHT: THE CONSTRUCTION OF NEW SUBDIVISIONS INCLUDES NOT ONLY LARGE SINGLE FAMILY DWELLINGS IN CLOSE-KNIT COMMUNITIES, BUT ALSO APARTMENT COMPLEXES WITH ALL THE MODERN CONVENIENCES. PHOTO BY DOUG MILLER.

MANY PARENTS CHOOSE TO RAISE THEIR FAMILIES IN THE RURAL SETTINGS OF THE VIRGINIA MOUNTAINS, WHERE THEIR CHILDREN CAN LEARN ABOUT NATURE OR THEY CAN SPEND TIME TOGETHER IN THE PEACEFULNESS OF THE COUNTRY. PHOTO AT LEFT BY PETE LARKIN. PHOTO BELOW BY HANK EBERT.

NOT ONLY DOES THE ROANOKE COUNTY DEPARTMENT OF PARKS AND RECREATION SPONSOR YOUTH SPORTING ACTIVITIES, BUT ALSO IT PROVIDES ACRES OF PARKS FOR NEIGHBORHOOD COOKOUTS AND FAMILY PLAYTIME. PHOTO AT RIGHT BY DOUG MILLER. PHOTO BELOW BY DAN SMITH.

THE CITIZENS OF ROANOKE HAVE STRIVED TO CREATE A HEALTHY QUALITY OF LIFE FOR THEIR FAMILIES, BUT THEY ARE CONCERNED ABOUT THE WILDLIFE THAT INHABITS THE LOCAL REGION, AS WELL. THE ROANOKE WILDLIFE RESCUE PROVIDES TREATMENT AND CARE IN ORDER TO REHABILITATE ANIMALS SO THESE CREATURES CAN RETURN TO THEIR NATURAL HABITATS. PHOTOS BY DOUG MILLER.

RELIGION CONTINUES TO BE A
VITAL PART OF THE REGION,
AND CHURCH ORGANIZATIONS
ARE VERY ACTIVE IN LOCAL
COMMUNITIES FROM HOLDING
REGULAR WORSHIP SERVICES
TO HOSTING FESTIVALS TO
PERFORMING CONCERTS.
PHOTO BY TOMMY FIREBAUGH.

ROANOKE VALLEY IS KNOWN AS A WONDERFUL PLACE TO RAISE CHILDREN, BUT IT IS JUST AS ENJOYABLE TO THOSE IN THEIR GOLDEN YEARS. THE LOCAL GOVERNMENTS HAVE ESTABLISHED PROGRAMS AND ACTIVITIES TO ENSURE LONG, HAPPY LIVES FOR ALL OF THEIR CITIZENS. PHOTO AT LEFT BY MARLEN A. GRISSO. PHOTO BELOW BY DAN SMITH.

THERE IS NEVER A SHORTAGE OF
FESTIVALS AND ACTIVITIES FOR
THE RESIDENTS OF THE VALLEY.
THE TANGLEWOOD MALL
FESTIVAL ALLOWS PARENTS AND
CHILDREN TO ENJOY INDOOR
ACTIVITIES SUCH AS FACE
PAINTING, WHILE PLACES LIKE
THE CITY MARKET OFFER A
UNIQUE SHOPPING EXPERIENCE
FOR THOSE DESIRING FRESH
FRUITS AND VEGETABLES.
PHOTO BY DAN SMITH.

ABOVE: HOTEL ROANOKE, SITUATED IN ROANOKE CITY, IS AN HISTORIC LANDMARK THAT HAS ALWAYS CHARMED GUESTS, BUT NOW THE HOTEL IS A FULL-SERVICE CONFERENCE CENTER, EXTENDING ITS HOSPITALITIES TO ITS MOST SOPHISTICATED BUSINESS CLIENTS. PHOTO BY DAN SMITH.
LEFT: ROANOKE COUNTY AND THE CITY OF ROANOKE CONTINUE TO THRIVE IN THE DOWNTOWN AREAS WITH FESTIVALS AND CITY MARKETS FREQUENTED BY RESIDENTS AND VISITORS YEAR-ROUND. PHOTOS BY DAN SMITH.

8

C H A P T E R
E I G H T

Over the River and Through the Woods

By Christina Koomen Smith

Each route through the countryside offers a glimpse of the County and valley that harks to another day and time—that which has been and can still be for generations.

Photo by Doug Miller.

"I guess if we could have our druthers, we would turn back the clock and live the way we used to."
—Louise Garman, Catawba

More than two centuries have passed since the first European settlers began moving to the Roanoke Valley of Virginia, and the ensuing years have brought astonishing changes. Carved out of the then enormous county of Botetourt, which covered an area from Western Virginia to Lake Michigan, and officially chartered in 1838, Roanoke County has been transformed from a quiet farming and milling community into the epicenter of business and commerce in the region. Yet, beyond the boundaries of its eponymous city and neighboring Salem and Vinton, the rural essence of this once pastoral locality lives on.

Long before the Revolutionary War, the area that came to be called Roanoke was a crossroads for wildlife—deer, bison, and other creatures which were attracted to the salt marshes near what are now U.S. Highways 460 and 11. Native Americans hunted these animals along their migration routes, establishing the rugged north-south trails which would bring the early Scottish, Irish, and German immigrants from Pennsylvania and Maryland into the valley.

These eighteenth-century pioneers had a tradition of working the land, and the fertile soils around the salt licks, coupled with strong water sources and abundant trees, offered an ideal setting for the kind of self-sufficient agrarian lifestyle the Europeans favored. Row crops like hemp and wheat, corn and flax, and barley and beans were widely cultivated. Farmers raised cattle, horses, sheep, and pigs, as well as some poultry in varieties that are rare or extinct today. The Pippin apple was just one of several species of tree fruits grown in orchards throughout the area, and a wide variety of vegetables was produced to put food on the family table. Grain mills and sawmills were built to process wheat and timber, and a local woolen mill provided cloth for Confederate uniforms during the Civil War.

By the turn of the century, agriculture was still the mainstay of the region's economy. Roanoke County was a major provider of farm commodities throughout the state, and the arrival of the railroad in the 1880s improved the ability to ship products to market. But along with the railroad came heavy industry, as well as people in search of the jobs such industry provided, and the nascent City of Roanoke began to expand like a patchwork quilt through a series of annexations, which by the 1970s had increased its size nearly tenfold.

ABOVE: LOCAL FARMERS'
MARKETS IN ROANOKE AND
SALEM PROVIDE A VENUE FOR
THE COUNTY'S STILL BOUNTIFUL
HARVEST OF PRODUCE—
BENT MOUNTAIN CABBAGE,
FOR EXAMPLE, IS COVETED
NATIONALLY. MOST DAYS,
CITIZENS AND TOURISTS FLOCK
TO THE ROANOKE CITY MARKET
SQUARE OR SALEM FARMERS
MARKET FOR A TASTE OF
THE GARDEN. PHOTOS BY
CHRISTIAN MOODY.
RIGHT: SMALL, SCENIC PARKS,
CREATED BY CITIES LIKE SALEM,
PROVIDE PLACES FOR PEOPLE
IN COMMUNITIES TO COME
TOGETHER TO ENJOY THE
SIMPLICITY OF NATURE OR TO
REMINISCE ABOUT OLD TIMES.
PHOTO BY CHRISTIAN MOODY.

With the expansion of the urban areas over the years, agriculture in Roanoke County has been reduced to a fraction of its former dominance, from 40 percent of the County's total land area as recently as the 1960s to 16 percent by the late 1990s. Ironically, some of the most productive soils in the region are in the heart of the City of Roanoke, and the mountainous terrain in the rest of the County limits the number of acres that can be cultivated. Today, only a couple of dairy farms, a few hog farms, and a dozen or so orchards remain.

However, there are still close to 200 beef producers, plus a substantial annual hay crop, nurseries, and greenhouses. Even a few wineries have been added to the mix. Local farmers' markets in Roanoke and Salem provide a venue for the County's still bountiful harvest of produce (Bent Mountain cabbage, for example, is coveted nationally), now brought to town by truck rather than horse and wagon, and most days citizens and tourists flock to the Roanoke City Market Square or Salem Farmers Market for a taste of the garden.

Many rural families have roots in the County that extend for generations. Some live on the same land their forebearers did and have continued the same line of farming, while others have returned to the area to reclaim a piece of their history. As recently as the 1950s, families in the County could still make a living on the land, albeit under sometimes rustic conditions. Women, in particular, rarely worked off the farm, and children provided valuable help in doing the always extensive list of chores. People walked almost everywhere they needed to go, and a Saturday trip to town was an all-day occasion.

Today, most rural householders commute to jobs in Roanoke, Salem, Vinton, or even Blacksburg, but feel blessed to be able to trade the noise and lights of the city for stars and nature's solitude at the end of the day. For those who farm, mornings, evenings, and weekends are the times for feeding livestock, cutting hay, or working in the garden.

In the winter months, when the earth lies dormant, there are always fences to mend or tools to sharpen. The country is as ever a friendly place, where everyone waves at passers-by—including the ones they don't know.

Church remains a social and spiritual hub in the rural neighborhoods, and the local general store is still a place to meet and catch up on the news of the day. Residents regularly come together for barbecue dinners at the volunteer fire departments or civic group meetings at the nearest school or community center. A strong tradition of caring lives on in the rural neighborhoods as well. There is a sense of joining forces to do what needs to be done, whether it's to help a family in need, or to rally around a common cause.

Not surprisingly, one of the most critical issues for the new millennium is preserving the flavor of rural life in Roanoke County. And it's not just long-time residents who are speaking out on the County's behalf. Recent arrivals, some of whom are experiencing for the first time the wonder of seeing wildlife in the backyard or relishing the sense of privacy that comes from not being able to see the house next door, are among the most vocal defenders of the County's open spaces.

Even though the Roanoke Valley's current growth rate of less than one percent is modest by many metropolitan standards, those who've spent their lives in this part of Virginia have seen farms and woodlands disappear. Aerial photos of the region reveal the dramatic transformation of a sparsely built environment into a complex tapestry of urbanization. Archival documents from as far back as the 1920s speak to the need for prudent stewardship of the land, but the past few decades of rapid growth and change have intensified concern for the County's rural heritage.

The governing entities of Roanoke County have demonstrated both an increasing awareness of the need to protect the rural landscape and an active resolve to deal with the issue. The County government's 1998 Community Plan offers a comprehensive vision for managing the County's land resources as the new century unfolds. In addition to farmland, rivers and streams, forest resources, and mountain ranges—the hallmark of the greater Roanoke Valley—will all be the focus of intensive land-use planning strategies. Those include protective overlays, conservation easements, and cluster development. Developers, too, have frequently been responsive to requests that their plans be modified to preserve precious green space and scenic vistas.

The slow but steady growth of the urban center and suburban ring has challenged not just the landscape but also a way of life that persisted for more than 200 years. Nevertheless, country living has not disappeared so much as it has evolved with the times. Residents who can remember hauling water to the house from nearby springs appreciate the conveniences of modern technology. For old-timers and newcomers alike, Roanoke County at the dawn of the new millennium offers an appealing combination of metropolitan amenities and an abiding connection to the natural world, each experience just minutes away from the other.

Protecting a rural heritage while maintaining a healthy economy is a challenge facing every generation. Take a drive out Virginia 311 west of Salem. As you crest Catawba Mountain, the verdant sweep of the pastoral Catawba Valley spreads below like an impressionist tableau. Or climb Route 221 south of the city limits of Roanoke and watch the suburban scene recede into the distance until you find yourself in a sylvan wilderness on top of Bent Mountain. Or drive the 27 miles of the Blue Ridge Parkway that stretch from the Franklin County line to the hamlet of Bonsack, and enjoy vista upon vista of rolling pastures, rustic fence lines, and barns the color of driftwood.

Each route offers a glimpse of the valley that harks to another day and time—that which has been and can still be for generations. In Roanoke Valley, it is a challenge representing the essence of modern civilization. ■

EAST HILL CEMETERY IS LOCATED ADJACENT TO THE SALEM HISTORICAL SOCIETY, WHICH WAS FOUNDED IN ORDER TO RECORD AND PRESERVE THE RICH HISTORY OF THE AREA. PHOTO BY DAN SMITH.

As with any progressing region, farms and woodlands have disappeared, and protecting a rural heritage while maintaining a healthy economy is a challenge facing every generation. Photo above by Linda A. Turner. Photo at right by Dan Smith.

MANY RURAL FAMILIES HAVE ROOTS IN THE COUNTY THAT EXTEND FOR GENERATIONS. SOME LIVE ON THE SAME LAND THEIR FOREBEARERS DID AND HAVE CONTINUED THE SAME LINE OF FARMING, WHILE OTHERS HAVE RETURNED TO THE AREA TO RECLAIM A PIECE OF THEIR HISTORY. AS RECENTLY AS THE 1950S, FAMILIES IN THE COUNTY COULD STILL MAKE A LIVING ON THE LAND, ALBEIT UNDER SOMETIMES RUSTIC CONDITIONS. PHOTO AT LEFT BY HEATHER FROESCHL. PHOTO BELOW BY DAN SMITH.

ABOVE: GRAIN MILLS AND SAWMILLS WERE BUILT TO PROCESS WHEAT AND TIMBER, AND A LOCAL WOOLEN MILL PROVIDED CLOTH FOR CONFEDERATE UNIFORMS DURING THE CIVIL WAR. TODAY, THESE MILLS ARE INTERESTING ATTRACTIONS FOR THOSE TOURING THE BLUE RIDGE AREA. PHOTO ABOVE BY TOMMY FIREBAUGH. PHOTO AT RIGHT BY LINDA A. TURNER.

LEFT: ROANOKE COUNTY HAS BEEN TRANSFORMED FROM A QUIET FARMING AND MILLING COMMUNITY INTO THE EPICENTER OF BUSINESS AND COMMERCE IN THE REGION. YET, BEYOND THE BOUNDARIES OF ITS EPONYMOUS CITY AND NEIGHBORING SALEM AND VINTON, THE RURAL ESSENCE OF THIS ONCE PASTORAL LOCALITY LIVES ON. PHOTO BY DAN SMITH.

FOLLOWING PAGE: THE BLUE RIDGE PARKWAY, WHICH STRETCHES FROM THE FRANKLIN COUNTY LINE TO THE HAMLET OF BONSACK, PRESENTS AN ENJOYABLE VISTA OF ROLLING PASTURES, RUSTIC FENCE LINES, AND BARNS THE COLOR OF DRIFTWOOD. PHOTO BY DOUG MILLER.

THE SLOW BUT STEADY GROWTH OF THE URBAN CENTER AND SUBURBAN RING HAS CHALLENGED NOT JUST THE LANDSCAPE, BUT ALSO A WAY OF LIFE THAT PERSISTED FOR MORE THAN 200 YEARS. NEVERTHELESS, COUNTRY LIVING HAS NOT DISAPPEARED SO MUCH AS IT HAS EVOLVED WITH THE TIMES. PHOTO BY DOUG MILLER.

PHOTO AT LEFT BY DAN SMITH.
MIDDLE AND BOTTOM PHOTOS
BY DOUG MILLER.

FOLLOWING PAGE: FOR
OLD-TIMERS AND NEWCOMERS
ALIKE, ROANOKE COUNTY AT
THE DAWN OF THE NEW
MILLENNIUM OFFERS AN
APPEALING COMBINATION OF
METROPOLITAN AMENITIES AND
AN ABIDING CONNECTION TO
THE NATURAL WORLD, EACH
EXPERIENCE JUST MINUTES AWAY
FROM THE OTHER. PHOTO BY
DOUG MILLER.

CELEBRATE 2000 PHOTO CONTEST

As part of the celebrations for the Year 2000, Roanoke County held a photo contest and encouraged Valley residents to "take their best shot at Y2K." Photos were taken in Roanoke County between April 1, 1999 and March 31, 2000, and the contest was judged by a team of photography professionals, historians, and college professors. The winners of the contest are featured in this book, and the pictures represent the different facets of Roanoke County life at the turn of the century.

Celebrate 2000 Photo Contest Judges:

Dr. Norma Jean Peters
Dr. Robert Sulkin
Dr. Elizabeth Heil
Stephanie Klein-Davis

PHOTO BY MITCHI
WATSON MANKIN.

PHOTO AT RIGHT BY MICHAEL
HENRY. MIDDLE PHOTO BY EDNA
CRABBERE. BOTTOM PHOTO BY
MARLEN A. GRISSO.

PHOTO BY ELLEN SUE HATCHER.

Top photo by Buddy Wells.
Photo above by Edna
Crabbere. Photo at right by
George Warner.

TOP PHOTO BY BUDDY WELLS.
PHOTO ABOVE BY BUDDY
WELLS. PHOTO AT LEFT BY
ALICE AUSTIN.

PHOTO AT LEFT BY
BUDDY WELLS. PHOTO BELOW
BY HANK EBERT.

PART TWO

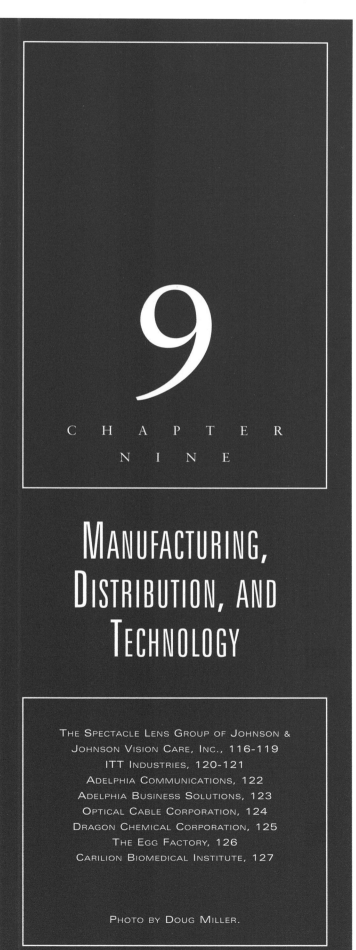

9

CHAPTER
NINE

MANUFACTURING, DISTRIBUTION, AND TECHNOLOGY

PHOTO BY DOUG MILLER.

THE SPECTACLE LENS GROUP OF JOHNSON & JOHNSON VISION CARE, INC.

The Spectacle Lens Group of Johnson & Johnson Vision Care, Inc., based in Roanoke, Virginia, is a wholly owned subsidiary of Johnson & Johnson. The Spectacle Lens Group has been developing what it anticipates to be the latest innovation in progressive addition lenses—the DEFINITY 2™ Lens, which will offer a distinct advantage over other progressive lenses. Manufactured with an exclusive, precision technique that distributes the vision prescription on the front and the back of the lens, the DEFINITY 2 lens is being developed to reduce peripheral blurriness often associated with progressive lenses and provide a wider field of clear vision for the wearer.

To house the revolutionary manufacturing technique required to perfect the DEFINITY 2 lens, the company has built a multi-million dollar facility in northwest Roanoke. The goal of the new facility is to create a state-of-the-art, high-speed manufacturing plant that will handle the anticipated demand, while making each DEFINITY 2 lens on an as-needed basis, suited to the individual's personal vision requirements. This unique manufacturing technology also is designed to help The Spectacle Lens Group serve customers promptly and accurately.

Before Johnson & Johnson purchased the company in 1997, it was named Innotech, founded by a Roanoke optometrist, Dr. Ronald Blum. Dr. Blum had a number of innovative ideas that combined technology with advanced polymer science to improve vision correction. Three years later, his vision was realized with the introduction of SurfaceCasting®, a patented process for in-office production of specialty eyeglasses.

Johnson & Johnson recognized Innotech's potential to revolutionize vision care, and purchased the company in March 1997. To reflect its new business alignment and focus, the company changed its name to The Spectacle Lens Group of Johnson & Johnson Vision Care, Inc., and established an even stronger presence in Roanoke. "The company is very pleased to be staying in Roanoke. The Roanoke Valley is one of the best kept secrets on the East Coast," said Val Brunell, president of The Spectacle Lens Group.

The Spectacle Lens Group estimates it will grow to approximately 600 people within three years of opening its new facility. To do this, the company anticipates creating jobs in marketing, research, and technical manufacturing, as well as in sales and management, and hopes to fill many of these positions with members of the local community.

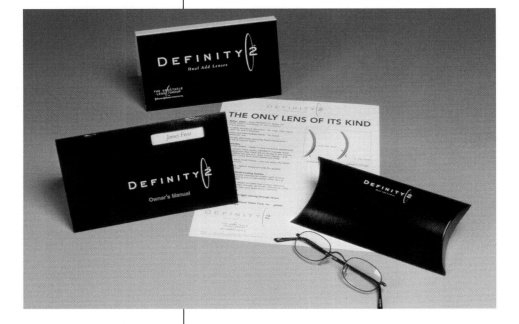

CUSTOMER SATISFACTION IS
EXTREMELY IMPORTANT TO THE
SPECTACLE LENS GROUP, AND
ITS CUSTOMERS' OVERWHELMING
SUPPORT HAS BEEN VERY
EXCITING. THE COMPANY'S
ON-SITE DISPENSARY IS USED
FOR EDUCATING AND ASSISTING
EYE-CARE PROFESSIONALS
ON BETTER METHODS OF
DISPENSING EYEWEAR.

This employment opportunity is great news for the approximately 228,000 residents of the Roanoke metro area, who already enjoy many of the benefits that earned the city a spot as one of *Kiplinger's Personal Finance Magazine's* 10 healthiest places to live in the United States. A recent Clark University study recognized Roanoke as having the most sustainable quality of life of any metro area in the Southeastern United States, and the 20th best in the country.

Among its many distinguishing qualities, Roanoke boasts thriving commerce, a low cost-of-living, and a burgeoning fine arts scene. Perhaps the feature that most drew the interest of Johnson & Johnson's subsidiary was the city's reputation for excellent, affordable, and accessible medical care. With its three major hospitals, a Veterans Administration facility, and satellite clinics throughout the area—including facilities with access to state-of-the-art medical technology—Roanoke is now a hub for health care.

Similarly, Johnson & Johnson has gained the public's respect by developing products of the highest quality such as Johnson's® Baby Shampoo and Band-Aid® Brand Adhesive Bandages, and continuing to improve health care with new pharmaceuticals and medical devices. The Spectacle Lens Group aims to uphold its parent company's reputation as a forward-thinking, innovative organization that is in touch with the needs of its customers, community, and employees.

The Spectacle Lens Group functions under the Johnson & Johnson belief to continually energize the company with new ideas, pioneering programs, and state-of-the-art equipment and human-resource practices. Such initiatives treat all Johnson & Johnson partners and employees with respect and dignity.

THE HIGHLY AUTOMATED
MANUFACTURING FACILITY
INCLUDES EQUIPMENT THAT IS
USED TO ASSESS THE QUALITY
AND ACCURACY OF EACH
MANUFACTURED PRESCRIPTION.

THE USE OF TECHNICAL
COMPUTERIZED EQUIPMENT
ASSISTS THE SPECTACLE
LENS GROUP IN PRODUCING
HIGH-QUALITY LENSES.

To further enrich the employment experience, The Spectacle Lens Group has extended many of Johnson & Johnson's innovative benefit programs that help its employees balance the demands of their lives, both inside and outside of the office. The Spectacle Lens Group hopes that its comprehensive benefits package shows Roanoke residents that the company is committed to being their employer of choice.

An example of this commitment is the company's LifeWorks® program, which provides personal and confidential consultation and referrals for employees who would like to better manage their commitments at work and at home.

In addition, The Spectacle Lens Group offers "Live For Life," a program that adds personal value to the work experience. This program helps employees keep healthy and fit.

The initiative will provide services such as on-site fitness trainers, occupational health nurses, support services for new mothers, and health screening programs for the company's workforce. The program also sponsors monthly seminars on health and wellness.

As part of Live for Life, The Spectacle Lens Group plans to build a dedicated fitness center at the new facility. In addition, the new facility will house a company store where employees can buy Johnson & Johnson products at discounted prices.

Another successful initiative The Spectacle Lens Group brings to Roanoke is Johnson & Johnson's Work and Family. This program has received national recognition for the way it focuses on the employee as a whole person. Under Work and Family, the company provides a rich variety of benefits including a resource and referral program, relocation services, family care leave, and a "nurture space" in its facility for new mothers.

UTILIZING ADVANCED LASER
RESEARCH TECHNOLOGY ALLOWS
THE COMPANY TO MANUFACTURE
ITS LENSES WITH PRECISION.

Rounding out its favorable corporate atmosphere is the company's dedication to act as a socially and ethically responsible enterprise. As explained by Ralph S. Larsen, Johnson & Johnson chairman of the board and CEO, "Johnson & Johnson has the focus, commitment, resources, and know-how. Most importantly, we also have a value system rooted in the Johnson & Johnson Credo. It doesn't mean that we will be perfect, but it does mean that we will do our very best to conduct business in a decent, fair, and honest way."

The Johnson & Johnson Credo also fosters a sense of responsibility for the communities in which its employees live and work, as well as to the global community the company serves. Johnson & Johnson donates to numerous charities and professional organizations in the local, national, and international arenas.

In addition, the company encourages and contributes to civic improvements, health care, and education. Johnson & Johnson has supported numerous programs across the world, including those in cancer research, infant health awareness, continuing medical education, wildlife preservation, disaster relief, and minority and women business enterprises.

By aligning itself with the values of Johnson & Johnson, The Spectacle Lens Group is following in the footsteps of its parent company and has become a valuable asset to the Roanoke region. The Spectacle Lens Group of Johnson & Johnson Vision Care is located at 2797 Frontage Road, Roanoke, Virginia 24017. ■

DEFINITY 2™ is a trademark of Johnson & Johnson Vision Care, Inc.

ITT INDUSTRIES

Virginia's Technology Corridor is so named because of businesses and educational institutions located along its path that embody technological advancement. One such business is ITT Industries' Night Vision Division. Although its location along Plantation Road— near I-81—has not changed since 1959, both the business and the technology have evolved dramatically during that time.

ITT Industries Night Vision is a world leader in the development and production of night vision equipment for military and commercial applications. It has experienced numerous changes over the past 40 years—changes in customers, product offerings...even changes in the Division's name. However, throughout its evolution, ITT has continued to focus on the development and advancement of imaging technology.

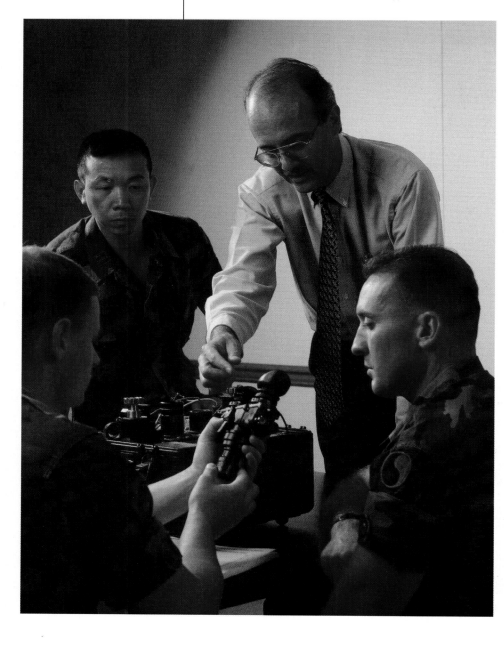

ITT's core strength lies in its ability to consistently develop and produce image intensifier tubes—in high volume—that surpass the performance of other tubes worldwide. The image intensifier tube is the heart of a night vision product. It gathers light present in the night sky, but not visible to the unaided eye, and intensifies it to a level of brightness that the human eye can easily see under dark conditions.

Producing such a device requires more than 400 separate process steps. Any variable along the way can affect tube performance, if not totally destroy the tube. In order to ensure product integrity and process consistency, ITT has invested in employee training and quality programs—such as statistical process control (SPC) and Taguchi methodology— and recently has launched a company-wide Value Based Six Sigma (VBSS) program.

During the 1960s and 1970s, various technological advancements defined the progression of image intensifier technology from Generation (Gen) 0 through Gen 3. With each advancement, night vision devices became lighter, less bulky, and easier to use. Most important, product performance improved significantly with each generation.

ITT established itself as the leader in Gen 3 development and production during the late 1980s. Through the 1990s the Roanoke Division consistently received the maximum allowable percentage of U.S. military contracts awarded for Gen 3 night vision devices.

In keeping with its leadership reputation, ITT recently introduced a new Gen 3 tube that surpasses the performance of all of its predecessors. Referred to as the Pinnacle™, this tube provides image quality and reliability that is superior to any other tube now available in the industry. Gen 4 tubes are now in final development and soon will enter production for contract deliveries.

The Roanoke division's number-one customer traditionally has been the U.S. Army. However, it also supplies night vision equipment to the U.S. Air Force, Navy, Marine Corps, and Special Forces. Its product line includes infantry goggles, aviator goggles, pocket scopes, weapon sights, accessories, and image intensifier tubes.

As the leading night vision supplier for the U.S. military, ITT also has earned the confidence of many international customers. International business growth was the impetus behind ITT's $20 million facility expansion during 1998. The resulting 3-story building increased the Division's total manufacturing area to more than 200,000 square feet.

While its international business continues to grow, restrictions do exist. ITT's export of high-performance night vision devices is highly regulated. The U.S. State Department must review every request for export. Only U.S. allies (NATO countries, plus Korea, Japan, Australia, Israel, and Egypt) are readily approved.

In addition to pursuing U.S. and international military markets, ITT has made the transition into commercial/consumer markets. Law enforcement and security personnel represent ITT's largest non-military customer base for night vision. In addition to supplying night vision products and accessories, the Roanoke division provides law enforcement officers several options for night vision training. It also actively supports the International Association of Chiefs of Police (IACP) and sponsors the IACP's annual Community Policing Award.

Consumer interest in night vision products exists primarily in smaller niche markets. These include boating, outdoor recreation—such as hiking and camping—and wildlife observation.

Being the leader in any industry requires the flexibility to respond quickly and easily to market dynamics while continuing to provide best value to the customer. ITT stands ready to meet that requirement as imaging technology moves to a new dimension: the merging—or fusing—of image intensification with heat sensing.

ITT Industries' Night Vision Division is committed to designing and manufacturing products that not only last for a lifetime, but also safeguard the lives of the people who use them. Such commitment typifies the corporate tagline: *Engineered for Life*. ∎

WHETHER FOR WORK OR FOR PLEASURE, BOATERS AND FISHERMEN NOW CAN EASILY NAVIGATE THEIR FAVORITE WATERWAY AT NIGHT—THANKS TO ITT.

ITT'S NIGHT VISION TECHNOLOGY, ORIGINALLY DEVELOPED FOR THE MILITARY, ENABLES POLICE AND SECURITY OFFICERS TO DETECT CRIMINAL ACTIVITY, EVEN UNDER THE DARKEST SITUATIONS.

ADELPHIA COMMUNICATIONS

Since its founding in 1952, Adelphia Communications has been committed to technological innovation and an ongoing concern for its customers. Adelphia has historical roots that extend deep into the origins of the cable television industry. John Rigas, while working as a management engineer and owning and operating a small movie theater in Coudersport, Pennsylvania, decided to buy his first franchise for a mere $100. The next year he took steps towards constructing and operating a cable television system.

As a pioneer in the industry, he recognized the potential that cable had to enhance the lives of people who lived far from the nation's urban centers. Together with his brother,

Gus, John Rigas spent the next two decades slowly building his "Community Antenna Association" into a respected cable operation.

In 1972, the company was formally incorporated under the name "Adelphia," derived from the Greek word for "brothers." By 1999, Adelphia had passed the five million-customer milestone for its Cable Entertainment.

A "clustering" approach to cable systems acquisitions has allowed for greater efficiencies in product expansion, service and marketing. Adelphia is now the dominant cable provider in south Florida and western New York, as well as the largest cable operator in the Los Angeles metropolitan area. The company also operates significant clusters of cable systems in sections of New England, Virginia, Pennsylvania, and Ohio.

Adelphia retains commitments to prompt, professional customer service and community involvement—two concepts at the very foundation of the company's success. Adelphia's professionally staffed customer service centers operate 24 hours a day, 7 days a week and can be reached toll-free from anywhere within Adelphia's service area.

Despite its enormous growth, the Adelphia of today holds much in common with the tiny operation of the 1950s. Throughout its systems, Adelphia has established a solid reputation as a good corporate citizen, supporting community events and charitable causes. Many Adelphia employees live in the communities they serve and are active in local affairs, serving as leaders of youth organizations, Chamber of Commerce officers, and enthusiastic volunteers. Adelphia's commitment to community development in the Roanoke Valley has also been reflected by the financial support of many worthwhile causes. ■

MR. JOHN RIGAS, CHAIRMAN, PRESIDENT, AND CEO, ADELPHIA COMMUNICATIONS CORPORATION, AND CHAIRMAN AND DIRECTOR, ADELPHIA BUSINESS SOLUTIONS.

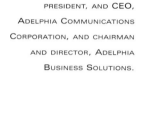

IN MAY 2000, ADELPHIA RAISED THE BAR FOR CORPORATE CITIZENSHIP IN SOUTHERN VIRGINIA. THE COMPANY RAISED $2,165 FOR THE VIRGINIA BAPTIST CHILDREN'S HOME AND FAMILY SERVICES IN SALEM BY ASKING CUSTOMERS TO MAKE DONATIONS IN LIEU OF THE NORMAL CABLE INSTALLATION FEE. PICTURED FROM LEFT: FRONT ROW, DARLENE NAPIER, DIANE MEADOWS, TRUDY McNEW. SECOND ROW, NANCY HALL; JENNIFER MARTIN, VIRGINIA BAPTIST PUBLIC RELATIONS; LYNN AMBROSIO; TERESA DEISHER. BACK ROW, JAN CLAYTON, ASSISTANT DIRECTOR OF DEVELOPMENT FOR THE CHILDREN'S HOME; LON CARRUTH, GENERAL MANAGER OF SALEM/TROUTVILLE/BLACKSBURG.

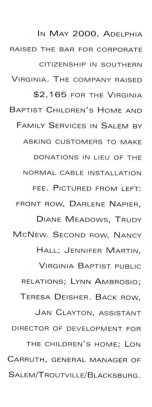

ADELPHIA BUSINESS SOLUTIONS

Not only is Adelphia a leader in the cable industry, but through its subsidiary, Adelphia Business Solutions, it has established itself as one of the premier communications providers to the business community.

The core of Adelphia Business Solutions is its advanced fiber optic network through which it delivers to Southwest Virginia a wide range of services including local voice, long distance, enhanced data, Internet access, and messaging services. These sophisticated services allow Adelphia Business Solutions to meet the needs of its business customers more completely and enhance its position as a single source communications provider.

The world is a much different place than it was when John Rigas strung his first television cable across the landscape of north central Pennsylvania. Throughout almost a half-century in the telecommunications business, Adelphia has prided itself on maintaining excellent relations with its customers, franchise authorities, and community leaders.

Adelphia is committed to pursuing its mission as a full-service communications operator offering advanced video, voice, data, and security to all of its service areas.

Adelphia is excited about the growth opportunities in the future and remains focused on strengthening its position as a key player in the communications arena. For more information please contact 540-342-5070. ■

LOCAL CUSTOMER CARE REPRESENTATIVES ARE AVAILABLE 24 HOURS A DAY, 7 DAYS A WEEK TO QUICKLY RESPOND TO CONSUMER NEEDS.

OPTICAL CABLE CORPORATION

stablished in 1983, Optical Cable Corporation manufactures and markets a broad range of fiber-optic cables for high bandwidth transmission of data, video, and audio communications. In 1996, Optical Cable Corporation undertook its own public offering to be listed on the NASDAQ National market, symbol OCCF.

COMPUTERIZED
FIBER-OPTIC CABLE
MANUFACTURING MACHINES.

Today, approximately one quarter of Optical Cable Corporation's sales are with international customers in more than 70 countries, and the company is one of the three largest producers of fiber-optic cables for LAN and data communications applications in the United States.

From its inception, Optical Cable Corporation pioneered the use of military tactical fiber optic cable technology. The company used advanced manufacturing techniques to offer new fiber-optic-cable designs specifically engineered for the requirements of moderate-distance, local area network installation environments.

As the market for fiber-optic cables has continued to advance and grow over the years, Optical Cable Corporation has stayed at the front edge of this state-of-the-art technology by designing custom fiber-optic cables to meet its customers' changing requirements.

Unlike some of Optical Cable's competitors, who manufacture both copper and fiber-optic cables, it specializes in manufacturing the highest quality and cost-effective, tight-buffer fiber-optic cables on the market. This means that each individual optical fiber has precisely applied layers of materials for physical and mechanical protection to preserve the optical qualities of the fibers over the design life of the product.

Optical Cable is easily able to customize its products to meet customers' specific requirements in situations where an off-the-shelf product may not be exactly what the customer needs.

Robert Kopstein, chairman, president, and chief executive officer, explains: "Understanding the requirements of our customers has led to our success in the past and will remain a key to our growth in the future. We believe that fiber-optic cable is a critical element in everyone's communications network and that only the rugged product should be used.

"Optical Cable Corporation prides itself on having one of the largest stock inventory variety and raw materials available for custom cable projects. Even our special, made-to-order fiber-optic cables are typically shipped in two or three weeks anywhere in the world."

Optical Cable Corporation remains enthusiastic about its long-term growth prospects. Its advanced technology, including unique computer automation hardware and software, provides a tremendous edge over the competition and allows Optical Cable to develop new products faster than global competitors. It has the ability to produce products with superior performance with significantly less labor content, and, most important, with quicker delivery to customers.

Optical Cable Corporation employs 200 people in the year 2000 at its 148,000-square-foot office and manufacturing facility in Roanoke County. It is driven by a tradition of leadership in technology, product performance, and customer service. ∎

INTERNATIONAL HEADQUARTERS
AND MANUFACTURING FACILITY
FOR OPTICAL CABLE
CORPORATION IN
ROANOKE, VIRGINIA.

DRAGON CHEMICAL CORPORATION

For more than 100 years, Dragon Chemical Corporation has been on the cutting edge of developing and manufacturing home and garden chemicals and fertilizers in the Roanoke Valley for use throughout the United States. Technology, innovation, quality, and a strong distribution base have contributed to the company's success in the ever-widening market place. Beyond that, Dragon Corporation takes pride in serving its customers. Dragon Corporation began in 1897 when the late James S. Harris established the J. M. Harris Company in the farmers' market area of Roanoke. The company originally manufactured two major product lines: home and garden insecticides and dog food. The company began selling its products under the names of "Blue Dragon" and "Star Dog Ration." The products were marketed through retail, seed, feed, and grocery dealers in Virginia, Ohio, and Tennessee.

Ernest W. Rose Jr. purchased and incorporated the company in 1956, operating it as a closely held, family-owned business. He soon restructured the company, eliminated the dog food portion of the business, and focused the company on selling quality home and garden chemicals and fertilizers.

In 1965, the company's name was changed to Dragon Chemical Corporation. James C. Wilson—Rose's son-in-law—was named president and became instrumental in directing the company's Dragon brand focus toward independent, full-service dealers. During this time, the Dragon brand developed into a full line of home and garden chemicals and fertilizers with more than 95 products sold through two-step distribution throughout the eastern and central regions of the United States.

In 1998, Dragon was purchased by Burlington Scientific Corporation. Burlington added a complementary line of animal repellants to Dragon's line of garden products.

Each year, Dragon continues to look for and to develop innovative products and marketing strategies to make it easier, safer, and more efficient for consumers to use garden chemicals and fertilizers.

Today, Dragon is introducing some exciting new changes in retailer and distributor programs. These include attractive new packaging that features increased shelf impact with displays and point-of-purchase materials that are sure to be shopper stoppers. Dragon Chemical is also setting new standards in fill rates and services every day. These all help its customers set the pace in today's intensely competitive retail climate.

Dragon Chemical Corporation has come a long way since 1897 and will continue to grow and change as the marketplace demands. As seen in the past 100 years, Dragon has never been afraid of change. In fact, the company has been comfortable taking on new challenges lin both manufacturing and distribution.

The managers at Dragon believe that while it is important to view the past, they must focus on the future to meet the challenge of the coming months and years. Today, the company is producing the finest products in its history and its managers intend to remain positioned to succeed in the ever-changing marketplace. ∎

THE EGG FACTORY

The Egg Factory is a company dedicated to the development of potential significant commercial innovations. The Egg Factory's focus is on originating, creating, developing, and managing substantial and/or transformational innovations from ideas through pre-market entry. The Egg Factory's end goal is to see these opportunities commercialized primarily by selling or licensing them to global companies.

THE EGG FACTORY FILLS THE CORPORATE "GROWTH GAP"

Regardless of their size, companies are expected to maintain certain percentage growth increases in order to sustain satisfactory returns to shareholders. As a company grows larger, this creates an increasing challenge because the dollar growth needed to maintain a steady percentage growth rate becomes more substantial every year. As a result, most companies have a "growth gap" between their targeted revenue growth and the revenue growth they are able to achieve through traditional means.

The Egg Factory closes this corporate "growth gap" by supplying substantial and transformational innovations to large global companies.

THE EGG FACTORY HAS ESTABLISHED A WEB OF STRATEGIC RELATIONSHIPS

The Egg Factory leverages world-class relationships and alliances with some of the leading research laboratories, universities, and firms around the world to create an extended firm. The Egg Factory uses these relationships in an effort to have the leading experts in a given field co-develop its opportunities. The Egg Factory currently has relationships in North America, Europe, Asia, and the Middle East.

THE EGG FACTORY'S PRODUCT

The Egg Factory's end products are "Golden Eggs," which are developed, pre-commercialized proprietary innovations that The Egg Factory believes will have the potential of achieving $1 billion plus of annual sales within five years after commercial launch by a global Fortune 500 company. The "Golden Eggs" would be "Packaged," meaning that concept testing, working prototypes, market research, consumer testing, and business plans would be included as part of the product. The Egg Factory's business model is to sell and/or license these "Golden Eggs" to qualified corporate candidates.

THE EGG FACTORY'S ASSETS

The Egg Factory's primary asset is its "Knowledge Capital," which includes a combination of proven business and technology leadership along with extensive experience in the commercial innovation process. The Egg Factory leverages this knowledge capital to create and develop a diversity of large opportunities.

Innovations currently under both development and/or investigation have applications in areas such as: digital audio technology, consumer electronics, wireless communications, hand-held computing, the movie industry, agri-technology, in-flight entertainment, flat-panel displays, vision care, meteorology, consumer products, law enforcement technology, e-commerce, and industrial/commercial products. ∎

CARILION BIOMEDICAL INSTITUTE

Headquartered in Roanoke, the Carilion Biomedical Institute is an exciting new partnership between the Carilion Health System, the University of Virginia, and the Virginia Polytechnic Institute & State University (Virginia Tech).

Its mission:
• Strengthen biomedical research at its partner universities.
• Accelerate commercialization of research ideas into safe, superior health-care solutions for the world.
• Create opportunities for economic development in central and southwest Virginia to improve the quality of life in the region.

Founded by a $20 million grant from the Carilion Health System, the Carilion Biomedical Institute has created a unique program to transform research into commercial results.

Research ideas are submitted to the Institute's university research centers. Selected projects receive seed funding for scientific and technical feasibility studies. Each project is carefully reviewed for relevance to today's health-care needs.

The Institute then identifies potential products within these projects and their market possibilities are evaluated. Finally, business plans are composed to rapidly commercialize these products through strategic business partnerships for production and distribution.

At each step in the process, programs that can not be developed within a 3 to 5 year period are encouraged to seek further basic research funding outside of the Institute.

The Carilion Biomedical Institute currently funds the Medical Automation Research Center (MARC) at the University of Virginia and the Optical Sciences and Engineering Research Center (OSER) at Virginia Tech. Teams of scientists from both universities work through their centers and with each other to conduct basic biomedical research.

Samples of current research activities include:
• Easy to use, non-invasive, inexpensive instruments to measure and automatically record patients' vital signs.
• Eldercare devices and robots, as well as overall living environments, to assist the disabled and elderly to remain in their own homes.
• Automated devices to speed the development of new DNA-based diagnostic and treatment programs.
• Low-cost tests for hereditary dispositions toward serious life threatening diseases.
• Less invasive, easier to use fiber-optic instruments for diagnostic, treatment, and surgical intervention in the body, as well as new applications for these instruments.
• New coating materials for artificial devices that have to be inserted into the body that prevent rejection by the body's own immune system.

As these university research centers mature, the Carilion Biomedical Institute may open additional centers. These centers will promote new facets of biomedical research and strengthen southwest Virginia's role as a biomedical technology leader. ■

A CBI-SPONSORED OPTICAL SCIENCES AND ENGINEERING RESEARCH CENTER (OSER) SCIENTIST AT VIRGINIA TECH INSTRUCTS HIS GRADUATE STUDENT IN THE USE OF A LASER IN ELECTRO-OPTIC EFFECT MEASUREMENT TECHNIQUES FOR BIO-CHIPS.

A CAD DRAWING OF AN AUTOMATED BIOLOGICAL SPECIMEN BANK TO PROCESS AND STORE UP TO HUNDREDS OF THOUSANDS OF DNA, PROTEIN, AND PLASMA SPECIMENS DESIGNED BY THE CBI-SPONSORED MEDICAL AUTOMATION RESEARCH CENTER (MARC) AT THE UNIVERSITY OF VIRGINIA.

10

C H A P T E R

T E N

TRANSPORTATION

AND

COMMUNICATIONS

PHOTO BY DAN SMITH.

THE ROANOKE TIMES

In 1886, when the first issue of *The Roanoke Times* emerged from a hand-powered press, the city of Roanoke, with a population of 6,000, was only a few years old. The beauty of the area, the accessibility by railroad, and the strategic location midway between Maryland and Tennessee made the Valley a popular destination and Roanoke a fast-growing new city. In the span of years since *The Roanoke Times* was born, the paper has emerged today as one of the nation's largest 200 newspapers. The newspaper, located in downtown Roanoke across from City Hall, has a bureau in the New River Valley and is the leading newspaper in southwestern Virginia. With a daily circulation of over 100,000, *The Roanoke Times* is rated in the top five percent of daily newspapers for metro penetration nationwide. Distributed in 19 counties, the newspaper has a Sunday circulation of 117,000.

The newspaper, originally titled the *The Roanoke Times*, served the citizens of the Roanoke Valley with a morning edition, chronicling the daily history of their lives, work and world. In 1909, a group led by Junius Fishburn, a prominent Roanoke citizen, purchased *The Roanoke Times* and an afternoon paper, the *Evening News*. Four years later, they bought a paper called the *Evening World* and combined it with the *Evening News* to form *The World-News*. In 1977, *The World-News* merged with *The Roanoke Times* to become *The Roanoke Times & World-News*. Both a morning and afternoon edition of *The Roanoke Times & World-News* were published until 1991 when the afternoon edition ceased publication. The World-News was dropped from the masthead of the newspaper in 1995, and the newspaper came to be known officially as *The Roanoke Times*.

The Roanoke Times was purchased in 1969 by its current owner, Landmark Communications, a privately held media company based in Norfolk, Virginia, that owns community newspapers in 11 states, including *The Virginian-Pilot* in Norfolk and the *News & Record* in Greensboro. Landmark is also the parent company of *The Weather Channel* and weather.com.

The Roanoke Times publishes three editions daily: one in the metro area, one in the farthest reaches of its circulation area, and another in the New River Valley. The New River Valley edition, which includes news and information from *The Roanoke Times'* metro edition, features content targeted to Blacksburg, Christiansburg, Radford, and surrounding counties.

The on-line edition of *The Roanoke Times*, roanoketimes.com, features the news and information found in the daily print editions, plus midday news updates; links to national and international news through the Associated Press; The Gamezone, where the latest Virginia Tech and UVA sports stories and stats can be found; and a searchable archive of articles in *The Roanoke Times*, including obituaries from 1900 through today.

The Roanoke Times offers another on-line site, roanoke.com, a interactive on-line community for residents of western and central Virginia. A resource for entertainment, weather, local events, business, and sports, features of roanoke.com include exclusive columnists, on-line yellow pages, Web hosting, custom Web design, "Our Town" Community Guide, BidZilla, Blue Ridge Careers, Blue Ridge Business netWORK, and a link to roanoketimes.com.

While covering everything from international events to local news, *The Roanoke Times* also offers a variety of engaging products for its readers. Those include: *Neighbors*, a zoned community news tabloid that is delivered on Thursdays to subscribers in Roanoke, Roanoke County, Salem, Vinton, Botetourt, and Craig County; *Current*, a community-oriented tabloid appearing Tuesday through Sunday in the New River Valley edition; *Current Real Estate*, appearing every Sunday in the New River Valley edition featuring homes for sale and rental properties in the New River Valley; *Jobs Weekly*, available every Monday free of charge through rack locations and providing a summary of employment classified ads; *Spectator*, a Saturday insert that provides full television listings for the entire week; *Homes Plus*, a zoned real-estate tabloid produced twice a month in conjunction with the Roanoke Valley Association of Realtors; *NewsFun*, a mini-newspaper printed just for children that is found in the main section of the paper on Mondays during the school year; and *Menu Guide*, a special advertising tabloid produced quarterly listing area restaurant menus.

The Roanoke Times' parent company also publishes two local magazines, the *Blue Ridge Business Journal* and the *Roanoke Valley Sports Journal*. The *Blue Ridge Business Journal* is a bimonthly publication covering news, trends, and people in the region's business community. *The Business Journal* is distributed to its subscribers and is available through

WITH THE SUPPORT OF *THE ROANOKE TIMES*, THE VALLEY ENJOYED THE MUSIC OF THE WORLD-RENOWNED HARLEM GOSPEL CHOIR IN A PERFORMANCE TO BENEFIT THE DOWNTOWN MUSIC LAB. PHOTOGRAPH BY STEPHANIE KLEIN-DAVIS.

Literacy Volunteers of America Book Sale, The Downtown Music Lab, Dickens of A Christmas, First Night Blacksburg, and the Blue Ridge Garden Festival. Annually, *The Roanoke Times* gives over $500,000 to the Roanoke Valley community. Roanoke Times employees are an active voice in the community as well, raising funds for the United Way and serving as volunteers on boards for Roanoke Area Ministries, the Boys and Girls Club, United Way, Junior Achievement, and the YWCA, among others.

The Roanoke Times has

regional newsstands. *The Roanoke Valley Sports Journal* features high school, local, professional, and semi-professional teams, recreational activities, as well as sports columnists. It is a free monthly publication distributed through 200 rack locations within the region.

Along with the many features and products *The Roanoke Times* offers its readers, the paper is also committed to sharing its resources with the communities it serves. With the **Newspaper in Education** (NIE) program, *The Roanoke Times* promotes literacy and a love of reading to children and teenagers. NIE uses the daily newspaper as a learning resource tool for students in kindergarten through 12th grade. NIE provides educational subscription rates to schools and curriculum guides. The majority of NIE materials are compatible with the Virginia Public Schools Standards of Learning curriculum.

Music For Americans, hosted by *The Roanoke Times* and the city of Roanoke, is the premier Fourth of July celebration in the Roanoke Valley region. This evening of patriotic music and fireworks display is presented each Fourth of July at Victory Stadium and is attended by more than 20,000 people.

The Roanoke Times' **Good Neighbors Fund** was established to assist Roanoke Area Ministries, which provides emergency assistance to more than 3,000 families in the Roanoke Valley and surrounding areas. From Thanksgiving to mid-January each year, *The Roanoke Times* receives more than $100,000 annually in donations to the fund and runs stories on families helped by Roanoke Area Ministries.

Each year, **All-Timesland** awards are given by *The Roanoke Times* sports writers to recognize the athletic achievement of high school students throughout the paper's readership area. All-Timesland winners receive recognition in the sports pages during the school year and in a special tabloid insert at the end of the school season.

The Roanoke Times is also an active supporter of many community groups and activities including the

been widely recognized for its community and journalistic achievements. The newspaper has won the Virginia Press Association award for journalistic integrity and community service seven times, including five awards in the 1990s. *The Roanoke Times* has also been a finalist for the Pulitzer Prize three times; won a George Polk Award in Journalism, a National Headliners Award, a Dart Award for Excellence in Reporting on Victims of Violence, and several Southern Journalism Awards, among others.

Committed to providing comprehensive news coverage, engaging products for its readers, and a connection to the community, *The Roanoke Times* is excited about the future. Realizing the impact technology has on the future of the Roanoke region, *The Roanoke Times* launched in January 2001 a weekly technology report to examine high-tech trends, issues, and news in the Roanoke Valley region and beyond.

Although computerized printing technology has replaced the hand-powered press used to print the newspaper some 115 years ago, *The Roanoke Times* will continue to uphold the strong journalistic traditions established at its birth by chronicling the daily news of southwestern Virginia as well as important news and events from across the nation and the world. ■

THE MARKET SQUARE IS TRANSFORMED INTO A HOLIDAY OF YESTERYEAR AT DICKENS OF A CHRISTMAS, SPONSORED BY *THE ROANOKE TIMES*. PHOTOGRAPH BY STEPHANIE KLEIN-DAVIS.

WSLS, NEWSCHANNEL 10

The first television station to serve Central and Southwestern Virginia, Roanoke's WSLS Television, officially signed on the air December 11, 1952, nearly half a century ago. WSLS-TV was licensed by the Shenandoah Life Insurance Company, a Roanoke Valley business institution today, as one of Southwest Virginia's pioneer stations. WSLS signed on shortly after WTVR-TV in Richmond and WTAR-TV in Norfolk became active. The station's studios are at Third Street and Church Avenue in downtown Roanoke.

WSLS-TV is a station of firsts.

• It was the first station to offer full color television;
• First to telecast from a remote location;
• First to use videotape;
• First to originate a network program from the local station ("The Today Show");
• First to use electronic news-gathering equipment;
• First to receive network programming via KU satellite downlink; and
• First to broadcast network programming in stereo.

WSLS was purchased by Roy H. Park Broadcasting of Ithaca, N.Y., in October of 1969 and in 1997 it was sold to Media General Broadcast Group of Richmond, becoming Newschannel 10. An NBC affiliate since sign-on, Newschannel 10 continues its long association with the number-one network, strengthening its commitment of listening, responding, and interacting with the community to deliver the best in news, information, and entertainment programming to its audience.

WSLS-TV's commitment to the community is reflected in promoting its "Spirit of Virginia" slogan, which means getting involved and helping to benefit its viewers' lives in positive ways. It has a proven record of sponsoring and promoting major community organizations and events, all with the ultimate goal of benefiting many deserving non-profit groups. This is accomplished with on-air messages, heavy news coverage, and involvement of station managers, on-air talent, and other staff members.

WSLS-TV has also demonstrated it is prepared to mobilize when unexpected tragedies occur. It helped spread the community's "Spirit of Virginia" by organizing major relief efforts for victims of devastating tornadoes and other natural disasters. The station has served as a drop-off point for supplies and donations, as well as organizing volunteers and volunteer organizations to come to the aid of those in need.

WSLS Newschannel 10 will continue to invest in new technology, creative local programming, and experienced news professionals to bring local news, weather, and entertainment to the community. It will continue to report the news from a local perspective, emphasizing how the community is personally affected by certain events.

Most important, the region's oldest station will continue to lend a helping hand to make the community it calls home a better place to live. ■

LAWRENCE TRANSPORTATION SYSTEMS

"T"hinking outside the box" might seem like a contradiction in terms for a moving and storage company. But a progressive business philosophy, coupled with a tradition of quality customer service, has helped Lawrence Transportation Systems become a pacesetter in its industry.

Founded in 1932 by Weldon T. Lawrence Sr., the family company that started as a hauler of produce and furniture has grown over the years into one of the largest over-the-road transportation operations in the United States. The company became an affiliate of United Van Lines in 1942, which has enabled it to access major markets across the country. Through a series of purchases and expansions starting in

the late '60s, Lawrence Transportation has established branches in Charlotte, Winston-Salem, Greensboro, and Raleigh, North Carolina, as well as Charleston, South Carolina, and Waynesboro, Virginia. In the past decade, the company has gone from running an average of 15 to 20 trucks a day out of the Roanoke office to managing a fleet of over 300 power units, two-thirds of them company-owned.

Approximately 300 of Lawrence Transportation's 500-plus employees work here in the Valley. Based in Roanoke since its inception, the company moved its headquarters from within the city limits to the outskirts of town in 1995. The new 30-acre compound includes over 125,000 square feet of warehouse and shop space, plus some 20,000 square feet of office space housed in an elegant, rambling homestead with views of the Blue Ridge Mountains.

About half of Lawrence Transportation's business continues to be moving and storage, particularly for major corporate clients, but the company has added a significant interest in truckload freight, and also runs a warehouse and shop division. Such diversification is a big part of current president Weldon S. "Chip" Lawrence's vision for the company's future. While his competitors "tend to put all their eggs in one basket," Chip believes that branching out is the key to remaining strong in times of economic fluctuation and is actively seeking a new business venture to realize his goal of having four distinct but complementary divisions.

Lawrence Transportation recently launched one of the most innovative programs the moving industry has seen in a long time: Customized Alternative Pricing (or CAP). In the rush to gain a competitive edge following deregulation in 1980, companies began utilizing complex pricing systems based on discounts and surcharges that eventually led to gross inefficiencies in the business. By simplifying its pricing and reversing some of those inefficiencies, Lawrence Transportation has streamlined its moving practices, cut the amount of packing material it uses by up to 70 percent, and saved customers money, and yet has improved quality.

Another important change has been the transition to employee ownership, with the formation of an ESOP in 1997. The company's workforce now has a personal stake in its employer's future, and Chip reports that the highly successful program has had a direct, positive impact on Lawrence Transportation's bottom line.

Of course, the numbers have been speaking for themselves for quite some time. Revenues have increased from $600,000 in the early '70s to $14.5 million in the mid-'80s to almost $40 million in the year 2000. Annual growth has averaged around 20 percent per year for the past four years, and the once regularly-leveraged company currently has no debt and has enjoyed 80 consecutive months in the black.

Now in its third generation as a family business, Chip gives much of the credit to those who came before him. But he also gives credit to the stable business climate in the Valley itself. Not only has he consistently been able to attract good people with solid work values—he also feels that the Valley affords one and all a quality of life that is second to none. ■

LAWRENCE PROVIDES A WIDE RANGE OF MECHANICAL SERVICE FOR OUTSIDE CUSTOMERS AS WELL AS ITS OWN FLEET.

LAWRENCE HEADQUARTERS WITH TWO OF THE TRANSPORTATION DIVISION UNITS.

ROANOKE REGIONAL AIRPORT

Customer service and convenience have been the distinguishing factors of the Roanoke Regional Airport since its earliest days. The airport, which is owned and operated by the Roanoke Regional Airport Commission, is an engine for economic growth, a regional air freight center, and a place where vacationers and entrepreneurs get their plans off the ground.

When travelers land at Roanoke Regional Airport for business or pleasure, the streamlined approach to passenger service gets them in and out quickly. The terminal's two-level design keeps pace with the busy commuter. The ground level features ticketing, baggage claim, and support services. The upper level features easy access to airline gates, a lounge and restaurant, ATM, gift shop, data ports, and places where business travelers can catch up on paperwork.

Five car rental companies are located at the main terminal, offering everything from sporty to sophisticated automobiles. Other ground transportation services, such as taxi and limousine, are also available near the baggage claim area. In addition, parking is convenient and reasonably priced.

Roanoke Regional Airport's primary service area includes 16 counties in western and central Virginia and three counties in southern West Virginia. Each day, more than 90 flights arrive and depart, which gives travelers in western Virginia flexibility in making their plans, whether they are heading across country or abroad. Direct flights to major airline hubs throughout the eastern United States are offered by representatives of four major airlines, affording travelers easy connections to hundreds of destinations throughout the U.S. and the world.

Roanoke Regional Airport strengthens the economy of the area with more than its passenger services. Because of the airport's facilities and strategic location, a number of major overnight air freight carriers regularly serve the Roanoke Valley. This provides businesses with faster overnight deliveries and later pickup times.

Extensive general aviation services are also offered, including aircraft charter, flight instruction, refueling, routine maintenance, and heated hangar storage. More than 100 private and corporate aircraft are based at Roanoke Regional Airport. The general aviation services offer the right mix of personal attention and advanced capabilities necessary to establish an ideal home for both private and corporate planes.

The Roanoke Regional Airport Commission will continue its quest to enhance and expand aviation-related services in Roanoke in a manner, which will ensure that the passenger and the region will reap the benefits. Safety, customer service, and community remain the most important elements of the airport commission's mission. ∎

ARTWORK BY ALBERT PALEY.

PHOTO BY MARLEN A. GRISSO.

11

CHAPTER ELEVEN

BUSINESS, FINANCE, AND THE PROFESSIONS

PHOTO BY DOUG MILLER.

HAYES, SEAY, MATTERN & MATTERN, INC.

The Roanoke Valley experienced a metamorphosis in the last half of the 20th century. The region evolved from a relatively unpopulated and isolated area that generally made its living by railroading and agriculture, to a comfortably larger population with a sophisticated and diversified economy very much in the commercial mainstream of the state, nation, and world.

Hayes, Seay, Mattern & Mattern, Inc., (HSMM), the area's largest architectural-engineering-planning firm, not only grew and benefited from this evolution, but continues to be in the forefront as an agent of the region's changing face. No other planning and design organization has influenced the region's evolving look more than HSMM. The firm has designed signature projects that brought greater security, a healthier environment, and new jobs and opportunities to the entire region.

Traditionally, architects and engineers are "invisible" to the public, although their work forms an important yet overlooked part of daily life. Area residents may know the HSMM name, but they may not recognize how much the firm's work touches them every day. They also may be unaware of how HSMM's influence extends from Roanoke across Virginia and the mid-Atlantic region to the far corners of the world.

It wasn't always that way. The firm began modestly in Roanoke in 1947 with the association of four war-weary professionals. Architect Paul Hayes and electrical engineer Gilbert Seay, both of whom designed for the Navy in Norfolk, Virginia, during the War, joined forces with brothers Edward and Guilbert Mattern, civil engineers who spent WWII in uniform with the Army Corps of Engineers. Their first projects were predictably small until the men could build the firm's reputation.

With perseverance, long hours of hard work, and a dedication to good design, the four partners quickly elevated the firm to a position of growth and strength. By 1950, HSMM employed 100 engineers, architects, designers, and draftsmen.

The firm moved from a partnership to a corporation in 1988. By the time HSMM celebrated its 50th anniversary in 1997, the award-winning firm employed 450 technical and support personnel in nine offices along the East Coast, and was consistently ranked as one of the nation's leading design firms. Today, HSMM maintains a full-service staff of architects, interior designers, planners, multi-discipline engineers, and technical and support personnel in 10 offices in Virginia and West Virginia, the District of Columbia, and North and South Carolina. The firm provides comprehensive services through its major market divisions: Buildings, Justice, Healthcare, Science & Technology, Environmental, and Transportation. HSMM provides water resources management services through its Watershed Concepts division and communications consulting and engineering services through its subsidiary, CTA Communications, Inc.

HSMM President and CEO Cecil G. Doyle says, "We are proud, and rightfully so, of our contributions to the growth and well-being of the Roanoke Valley and beyond." "But," Doyle notes "our founders never let past success get in the way of building for the future." He counsels that "like the rest of society, HSMM has to change and grow with the times to flourish as a corporation."

This acceptance of change has been a hallmark of the firm's culture as it has helped put a new face on the nation's landscape. HSMM designed Virginia's first miles of interstate highway, and continues to be a significant force in highway and bridge design across the Commonwealth. Architecturally, the firm has led the region in medical and technical facilities design, from Roanoke's Community Hospital and the Veterinary School at Virginia Tech, to Johnson & Johnson's innovative manufacturing plant for its Spectacle Lens Group, as well as the first American assembly facility for Japan's Koyo Steering Systems. In recent years, HSMM designers have helped revitalize the heart of Roanoke's downtown. Through the Century Project, Center-in-the-Square, the Pedestrian Bridge, the Transportation Museum, the Railside Linear Walkway, and the Jefferson Center (a premiere performing arts venue), HSMM has played a key role in

HSMM OFFERS A WIDE VARIETY OF SERVICES TO HIGH-TECH RESEARCH AND MANUFACTURING CLIENTS MOVING INTO THE ROANOKE VALLEY, LIKE THE SPECTACLE LENS GROUP OF JOHNSON & JOHNSON VISION CARE, INC. HSMM PROVIDED COMPLETE PLANNING AND DESIGN SERVICES FOR THE GROUP'S NEW HIGH-TECHNOLOGY COMPLEX, AS WELL AS DUE DILIGENCE INVESTIGATIONS, PERMITTING, ENVIRONMENTAL ASSESSMENTS, COST ESTIMATES, AND MASTER SITE PLAN DEVELOPMENT. 3D RENDERING CREATED BY HSMM'S ANIMATION STUDIO.

transforming the downtown business district into a vibrant center for arts, entertainment, and shopping.

Taking the firm's helm at the dawn of the new millennium, Doyle has his, and HSMM's focus, on the future. He emphasizes, "The technological revolution of recent decades must blend with the creativity of our professional staff to continue to bring solid, cost-effective design solutions to society's ever-changing problems and challenges." One of the more intriguing applications of new technology with creativity is the firm's extensive use of computer-generated 3-dimensional animation and virtual reality techniques for engineering and architecture. These tools are quite useful for design teams and have the added advantage of letting clients "see" new buildings, highways, bridges, parks, or any project before construction ever begins. The client can even take a virtual tour inside a proposed facility, complete with furnishings, windows, lighting, and interior decorating.

HSMM's commitment to embracing advanced technology is also evident through comprehensive communications systems design at its CTA Communications subsidiary in Lynchburg, and in the marriage of computer technology with sophisticated hydrological engineering for cutting-edge water resource management at HSMM's Watershed Concepts in Greensboro, North Carolina.

HSMM's commitment to community improvement is also well documented in the region. One challenge faced and conquered was the firm's design of Roanoke County's massive Spring Hollow Dam and Reservoir, one of the largest roller-compacted concrete dams in the world. When discussions of the project began in the mid-1980s, HSMM contributed to the initial planning and worked closely with local officials to design a water resource that would safely serve the population well into the 21st century. The award-winning project was completed in 1994.

From the Center in the Square to Roanoke's Pedestrian Bridge, the Radford Arsenal to Rocky Mount's YMCA and Center for Applied Technology and Career Exploration, the Poff Federal Building to the Pentagon in Arlington and countless federal facilities around the world, HSMM's designers are at work.

Whether designing office buildings, justice facilities, hospitals, educational projects, or high-tech manufacturing facilities, sewage treatment plants, highways, bridges, or communications systems, HSMM continues to contribute valuable public and private additions to the economic, social, and commercial landscapes of Roanoke Valley and beyond.

While known for its contributions in architectural and engineering design, HSMM also maintains a high profile in the Roanoke Valley as a good corporate citizen. The firm and its many employees, in Roanoke and other cities, consistently support community organizations such as the United Way and Chamber of Commerce, and are active in many civic groups, including Kiwanis, Rotary, the Lions, and others. HSMM employees volunteer for a wide variety of charitable groups and give generously to the many communities the firm calls "home." ■

SPRING HOLLOW DAM AND RESERVOIR, LOCATED IN ROANOKE COUNTY, IS A TRUE ENGINEERING ACHIEVEMENT WITH ITS 243-FOOT-HIGH DAM AND 3.2 BILLION-GALLON RESERVOIR. HSMM ENGINEERS WORKED CLOSELY WITH LOCAL OFFICIALS THROUGHOUT THE PLANNING AND DESIGN PROCESS TO DESIGN A WATER RESOURCE THAT WOULD SERVE THE POPULATION FOR DECADES TO COME.

ALLSTATE INSURANCE COMPANY

K nown as "The Good Hands People," Allstate has built its reputation as a great American company by providing innovative products, offering excellent service to its customers, creating a solid value for its investors, and reaching out to communities to make them better places to live and work.

Founded in 1931 as part of Sears, Roebuck & Company, Allstate became a publicly traded company in 1993. At the time, its initial public offering was the largest in U.S. history. On June 30, 1995, it became a totally independent company after Sears divested its remaining share to Sears' stockholders.

As the nation's largest publicly held personal lines insurance company, Allstate is an industry leader. More than 39,000 employees and 13,000 agents across the globe provide 24-hour service, peace of mind, and assurance to their customers. Serving more than 14 million households' personal lines policies, Allstate is the second-largest insurer of automobiles and homes in the United States. Allstate offers a diverse range of life insurance, investment, and savings products to meet customers' changing needs and, as a result, is one of the fastest-growing life insurance and financial services companies in the industry.

In addition to its national reputation, Allstate has also captured a strong global presence. To stay competitive in a growing global economy, Allstate maintains international offices in Canada, China, Japan, Germany, and South Korea.

Regionally, Allstate is also a key player and strong economic force. Drawn to the Roanoke Valley for its strong work force, qualified work pool, and quality of life, Allstate

opened its first offices in downtown Roanoke in 1951 and has been one of the area's leading employers year after year.

Since that time, Allstate takes pride in being an organization committed to building stronger, safer communities. Whether selling a policy, quickly settling a claim, or partnering on a neighborhood rehab project, Allstate employees are active in the community as business people, as citizens, and as neighbors. Allstate has always believed that the key to its success is giving back to the community. Demonstrating this commitment, the Roanoke-based Allstate support center employees consistently surpass Allstate offices across the country in annual United Way donor participation. The local Allstate team also participates in such community outreach efforts as the March of Dimes, Juvenile Diabetes Foundation, the Relay for Life Cancer Walk, Junior Achievement, and the American Red Cross. In addition, Allstate sponsors a number of After Prom Parties for local high schools to promote automobile safety and remind youth about the dangers of drinking and driving.

The Allstate building off Va. 419 in Roanoke, known as the National Support Center, has been a local landmark since 1970 and now serves as the primary support center for the company's operations across the country. Allstate's 1,200 employees at this location handle more than two million phone calls per year, support approximately 13,000 agents in 49 states, and process policies for more than 14 million customers across the United States. In the Roanoke Valley, Allstate customers are represented by 18 professional agents.

Always a forerunner in innovative processes, Allstate strongly believes in providing pertinent information to its customers and largely relies on the most advanced technology to accomplish this goal. Allstate agents were among the first in the industry to use computers to process new business, produce quotes, and file on-the-spot claims. Allstate operates a company-wide, integrated Web-based system that allows employees to connect faster, share information, and respond to customers more effectively than ever before. Allstate's Worldwide Web site at www.allstate.com provides customers direct access to the most current information regarding Allstate's products and services.

Allstate's actions are aimed at one overarching goal: to serve and satisfy its customers. Its continued success is reflected in the dedication to excellence of its employees and agents.

Continually seeking and building new opportunities is part of Allstate's long range goal. As Allstate enters the 21st Century, the company is committed to building on its longstanding reputation for customer and public service, to make "being in good hands with Allstate" the only place to be. ■

NATIONAL FINANCIAL SERVICES, INC.

HELPING CLIENTS LEAVE A POSITIVE MARK ON THE WORLD

A tradition of integrity and a philosophy of putting the client first are the threads that have held National Financial Services, Inc., together for almost a century. The Roanoke-based financial services and consulting firm, which has branch offices throughout Virginia and in Kingsport, Tennessee, is a company that has made the creation, preservation, and transfer of assets its top priority since 1904.

According to Eddie Hearp, President of National Financial Services, Inc., the company had its beginnings as an insurance firm; however, the business has evolved and matured into a complete financial services firm. "We excel in retirement plan design, retirement distribution strategies, advanced estate planning strategies, as well as consulting in personal and business insurance, disability protection, long term care insurance, annuities, investment* products, and asset management.

National Financial Services is comprised of a diverse team of highly qualified specialists, available to advise clients in the areas of business succession and estate planning strategies, executive and employee benefits, 401K plans, IRA rollovers, and fee-based financial planning*. Investment* and asset management consulting are also among the most valued services made available to its clients.

Because each member of the consultant team has a specific area of expertise, clients benefit from the knowledge and experience of an entire team of specialists, whose goal is to help achieve and maintain the financial well being of their clients and their heirs. "In this industry, there are many firms that engage in the marketing of products through transactions. Our process is more consultative," says Hearp, "We want to know what are our client's goals, objectives, priorities, and dreams. We try to tailor our recommendations for each situation because we realize that one size does not fit all. We are also very conscientious about the recommendations we make to ensure they are appropriate for the inevitable changes in a client's life—variables such as financial issues, health changes, and tax law revisions. The relationship we have with our clients is not only professional; over time it becomes personal. Their goals become our goals."

EDDIE F. HEARP, CLU, CHFC, PRESIDENT OF NATIONAL FINANCIAL SERVICES, INC.

NATIONAL FINANCIAL SERVICES' DIVERSE TEAM OF HIGHLY QUALIFIED SPECIALISTS ALLOWS CLIENTS TO BENEFIT FROM THE KNOWLEDGE AND EXPERIENCE OF VARIOUS AREAS OF EXPERTISE, WHILE MAINTAINING A UNIFIED GOAL OF PROTECTING THE FINANCIAL SECURITY OF CLIENTS AND THEIR HEIRS.

While some stockbrokers and insurance agents engage in a single-layered, transaction-based business, National Financial Services takes a comprehensive approach. Its trained and professional associates believe families and business owners need someone who can provide a wide range of options. They understand their client's need to know what alternatives are available to them, and which options have the potential to yield optimum results. Every option is weighed to make certain that the recommendations given are in the best interest of the clients. "Our associates are proud of what they do. It is almost a mission," says Hearp. "Our feeling is that people do not care how much you know until they know how much you care."

At National Financial Services, Inc., the advisors are not interested in an immediate and single transaction. They are interested in building and maintaining relationships with their clients. If the degree of their client's loyalty is any measure, they have proven to be on target. Over 65 percent of National Financial Service's new business is generated through existing clients and many referrals come from the CPA, Attorney, Trust Officer, and existing clients.

Hearp, who co-authored "Family Wealth Counseling: Getting to the Heart of the Matter," has long believed that people who dedicate their professional lives to providing for their families should not have the bulk of their estate transferred to the Federal Government after their death. "I have been in the financial services industry for over 30 years. It has been my observation that the most vulnerable families are those who have never been through an estate settlement or who are still so busy creating or enjoying their wealth that they fail to plan," says Hearp. "Many people spend more time planning their vacations, than planning their estate. People do not plan to fail, they fail to plan."

The fact is most estates consist of a mixture of liquid and non-liquid assets. Estate transfer costs must be paid in cash, usually nine months from the date of death. Often times, the most liquid assets are extracted from the heart of the estate. As a result, the remaining non-liquid assets are sold at depressed prices to generate needed immediate cash.

It is the goal of National Financial Services, Inc., to steer its clients in the best direction through careful planning, and to keep families in their same or improved economic world. Often, this involves a family business successorship

plan, establishing wills, trusts, and gifting programs. Also efforts are made to redirect social capital to benefit a variety of worthy causes in order to reduce or eliminate estate taxes and other settlement costs.

Studies reveal that as baby boomers reach middle age and beyond, over the next 20 to 25 years, the intergenerational transfer of wealth in this country will surpass any comparable period in history. This economic transfer of wealth provides an unrivaled opportunity to fund non-profits, endow foundations, contribute to medical research, fund environmental programs, help the underprivileged, and to cast a shadow beyond the grave for many individuals and families.

National Financial Services works with its clients to grow their estate, provide for retirement, protect the estate created and to make a difference in the lives they will continue to touch long after they are gone. It is the mission of every associate at National Financial Services, Inc., to underwrite dreams and to protect tomorrows. National Financial Services Associates understand that, "Planning is a journey, not a destination." ■

*Eddie Hearp is a registered representative and investment adviser representative of Equity Services, Inc. Securities and investment advisory services are offered solely by Equity Services, Inc., member NASD/SIPC 4401 Starkey Road, Roanoke, VA 24014 (540) 989-4600. National Financial Services, Inc., is independent of Equity Services, Inc.

WHILE SOME STOCKBROKERS AND INSURANCE AGENTS ENGAGE IN A SINGLE-LAYERED, TRANSACTION-BASED BUSINESS, NATIONAL FINANCIAL SERVICES TAKES A COMPREHENSIVE APPROACH, PROVIDING FAMILIES AND BUSINESS OWNERS A WIDE RANGE OF OPTIONS.

NATIONAL FINANCIAL ADVISORS ARE NOT INTERESTED IN AN IMMEDIATE AND SINGLE TRANSACTION. THEY ARE INTERESTED IN BUILDING AND MAINTAINING RELATIONSHIPS WITH THEIR CLIENTS.

MARTIN & ASSOCIATES

Creative, client-responsive, and professional are a few words to describe Martin & Associates, a multi-disciplined architectural firm providing extensive design services to the industrial, educational, and commercial marketplace of the region. The firm maintains a strong client base, not only in the Roanoke Valley, but also throughout Virginia and adjacent states.

resulted in a $130-million capital-improvement program. The implementation of Phase I projects included a new high school, a new elementary school, major renovations at one of the existing middle schools, and smaller additions at several elementary schools within the Roanoke County school system.

Martin & Associates adheres to the highest standards of professional practice and holds a corporate membership in the American Institute of Architects. The firm's comprehensive "concept through completion" involvement in every project ensures that every client realizes the maximum value for the investment dollar. Along with this, the firm maintains a position of coordinating the services of all engineering consultants and providing the individual client with a responsive, dedicated, and knowledgeable management team.

In addition to the dedicated professional involvement exhibited by the entire staff, members of the firm are also involved in community affairs. One example of this is Ron Martin's commitment having served as President of the Back Creek Elementary PTA and the Valley Youth Hockey Association, in addition to currently serving as a board member to the Julian S. Wise Foundation and the Roanoke County Industrial Development Authority.

Total involvement is the key element, whether working on a design project or working within the community. Martin explains: "At Martin & Associates, we carefully listen to our clients, offer creative design solutions, and make sure everyone involved works as a team to accomplish the goal. Our greatest reward is client satisfaction." ■

PICTURED IS THE CONSTRUCTION (ABOVE) AND SITE PLAN (RIGHT) FOR A NEW HIGH SCHOOL IN BUENA VISTA, VIRGINIA. THIS 65-ACRE WOODED SITE, WITH A TOTAL ELEVATION CHANGE OF OVER 215 VERTICAL FEET, WAS PARTIALLY GRADED BY THE ARMY CORPS OF ENGINEERS. THIS WORK WAS PERFORMED AT MINIMAL COST TO THE CITY OF BUENA VISTA AND CONTRIBUTED "FILL MATERIAL" TO THE FLOOD REDUCTION PROGRAM BEING ADMINISTERED BY THE CORPS ALONG THE MAURY RIVER. TOTAL SITE DEVELOPMENT INCLUDES THE CURRENT HIGH SCHOOL LOCATION, PARKING, AND ATHLETIC FIELDS, ALONG WITH PRE-GRADING FOR A FUTURE MIDDLE SCHOOL AND COMMUNITY AUDITORIUM.

Originally established in 1979 as a partnership, the firm reorganized in 1983 as a professional corporation and became recognized as Martin & Associates. Ronald M. Martin serves as president of the firm, along with being a working member of the full-time architectural staff of seven. Martin & Associates offers its clients the convenience and security of a single-source contact, for all aspects of project development, providing broad services as well as personal service that clients appreciate.

Martin and Associates has provided creative design solutions for everything from educational facilities to industrial plants and manufacturing facilities to health-care facilities. Two of the firm's recent projects in the Roanoke Valley include the Joseph C. Thomas Alzheimer's Facility and the Roanoke City Police Department. In order to address the unique needs of these specific projects, outside consultants specializing in health care and public safety were added to the design team to ensure that the most advanced technology was incorporated into each project. In addition, on-site research was conducted to ascertain critical information from the client's management staff.

Martin & Associates has served clients in industry, commerce, education, medicine, and government. Evidence of the firm's success is reflected in the fact that 60 percent of its current business is for repeat clients. The firm is one of the most respected architectural firms in the region and has gained significant recognition for numerous projects throughout Virginia.

One example of the firm's impact in Roanoke County is the successful completion of a comprehensive facility study for Roanoke County Public Schools. The study was community-based and analyzed 28 individual school buildings, and

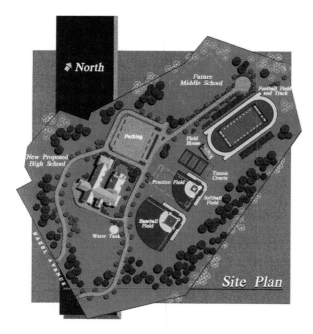

Site Plan

HILL STUDIO

In the professional practice of planning, landscape architecture, architecture, and preservation, Hill Studio emphasizes environmental sensitivity and historic integrity as cornerstones of its design process. A fundamental respect for these qualities is particularly appropriate in the Roanoke Valley, home to the firm and backdrop for many Hill Studio projects. The naturally scenic surroundings and cultural heritage of the Roanoke Valley present opportunities, challenges, and responsibilities when considering man-made intervention. Hill Studio plays a significant role in development projects throughout the region, exploring and implementing change through quality design and carefully planned actions.

The renovation of the historic Hotel Roanoke is a prime example of the firm's involvement in projects that recognize and value specific cultural and environmental attributes. For over a century, the Hotel Roanoke has been a symbol of southern hospitality and family life in the Roanoke Valley. As project landscape architects for the multi-client redevelopment group, Hill Studio provided the master site development plan for the early 1990s renovation of this 11-acre landmark hotel and grounds. Research turned up historic post cards, collected as family keepsakes, depicting the hotel and grounds through the years. The post cards inspired plans to recreate special landscape areas given up to accommodate the automobile in the early 20th century. An elliptical bowling green was the genesis of a present day space designed specifically to host wedding receptions. The chef's kitchen garden is another feature rooted in the past and reintroduced during the hotel renovation. Today, the Hotel Roanoke and Conference Center serves the region as an improved amenity and provides a signature place to celebrate long-standing and emerging traditions in keeping with the warm hospitality of the growing Roanoke Valley.

A project developed for Roanoke County further demonstrates Hill Studio's commitment to focus on appropriate environmental and historic context. The mountain ridges that grace the horizon of the Roanoke Valley are inherently challenging for site development. In 1997, Hill Studio led a

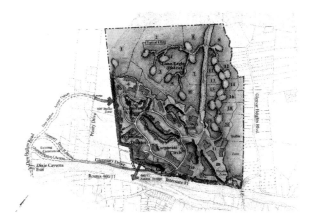

team of design professionals in developing a new vision for a business and manufacturing park nestled within the rolling topography of the region. As a result, the Roanoke County Center for Research and Technology was specifically created to cater to high technology and specialized businesses seeking a close association with a natural setting. Once the center is complete, only 250 acres of the 456-acre park will be devoted to the built environment, and the remainder will be left in outdoor spaces for approximately 5,000 employees to enjoy spectacular scenery, trails, and other amenities not usually associated with the work place. Hill Studio worked closely with neighboring residents, tailoring the concept plan to attract businesses the community could welcome and prosper alongside.

Both the Hotel Roanoke and the Roanoke County Center for Research and Technology necessitated the visionary leadership of public administrators and politicians. Site planning is capitalized upon in the firm's architectural achievement, evidenced by the new Mill Mountain Visitor Center, the award-winning affordable houses of Northwest Neighborhood Environmental Organization, and numerous downtown building renovations. Hill Studio develops the vision into meaningful places that respect the area's past and present, yet fit the long term goals for the future of the Roanoke Valley. ■

THE ATLANTIC MUTUAL COMPANIES

PREMIER PROVIDER OF INSURANCE

A Founded in 1842 on Wall Street, Atlantic Mutual is proud to be one of America's oldest and most well-regarded insurance companies and to have played a notable role in both American history and in the history of the insurance industry. Since its inception, Atlantic Mutual has insured some of the world's great ships, including the Titanic and the Andrea Doria. It has provided insurance for some of America's oldest and largest companies and for some promising technical start-up companies. Atlantic Mutual has also insured some of America's most beautiful and distinguished homes, museum collections, and public buildings.

Atlantic Mutual has always been visionary when it comes to foreseeing the role technology would come to play in the insurance industry: it was one of the first insurance companies to implement electronic data processing and the first insurance company to sell commercial insurance over the Web.

Today, Atlantic Mutual is a national insurer, licensed in every state and offering commercial, marine and personal property, and casualty insurance. Atlantic still operates on the same sound insurance principles that made it a leader in the insurance industry: prudent, independent underwriting judgement, prompt and ungrudging payment of just claims, and distribution of products through independent insurance agents and brokers.

ATLANTIC MUTUAL COMES TO ROANOKE

Following a long and careful search for a new site to house its growing computer operations, Atlantic Mutual finally chose the Roanoke Valley and officially moved in on May 11, 1970. At first handling only the company's back office operations, in 1978 the company's computer and data processing functions were relocated from New York. In the early '80s, Atlantic Mutual's Technology and Customer Service Division in Roanoke began to handle all commercial business rating, policy issuance, and policyholder services.

Built in 1978 and expanded in 1984, Roanoke's Technology and Customer Service Division is Atlantic Mutual's largest facility, home to almost 700 employees engaged in occupations crucial to the operation of a modern insurance company: software developers, IS network and systems administrators, technical support personnel, raters and policyholder services staff for commercial, personal, marine, and surety lines of business, and other operational and support personnel. Roanoke is also home to Atlantic Mutual's Affinity Program Marketing Center, a field office dedicated to writing and servicing large group commercial business, and to a national auto physical damage claims unit.

COMMITTED TO THE COMMUNITY

Atlantic Mutual believes in contributing to the communities in which it does business, a sentiment embraced by its Roanoke employees. Atlantic Mutual is one of the largest fundraisers for the United Way of Roanoke Valley, and Atlantic Mutual employees are also active in Junior Achievement, Child Abuse Prevention Council, Child Health Investment Partnership, Literacy Volunteers, and Meals on Wheels, to name just a few. Through scholarships and paid internships, Atlantic Mutual also supports several educational establishments in the Roanoke Valley, including Virginia Tech, Roanoke College, Virginia Western Community College, and Salem High School.

Providing outstanding service to policyholders, developing ground-breaking technological applications for the insurance industry, and giving back to the communities where it operates are the principles certain to guide Atlantic Mutual's Roanoke Technology and Customer Service Division into the 21st century. ■

A SUNNY SPOT FOR MEALS AND GATHERING WITH FRIENDS.

SINCE 1978, ATLANTIC MUTUAL HAS BEEN A ROANOKE VALLEY LANDMARK.

HARRIS OFFICE FURNITURE COMPANY INC.

H arris Office Furniture got its start in 1950 when Julius and Anne Harris, who ran a dry cleaning business, put a sign on the store's front door advertising some used office furniture. When customers showed a great interest, the Harrises began ordering truck loads of office furniture from government surplus and Harris Office Furniture Company Inc. was born.

At the time, they sold on a cash and carry basis.

In the fall of 1967, George Reimer joined the organization and eventually began managing the store. In the spring of 1976, George and Judy Reimer purchased Harris Office Furniture Company from Julius and Anne Harris. The first few years of their ownership continued to be walk-in traffic seeking used office furniture.

The Reimers had a keen sense of the changing markets and expanded into new office furniture. Today, Harris Office has the ability to furnish complete interiors, including systems furniture (more commonly known as cubicles). Harris Office employs two full-time designers who provide complete interior design consulting from efficient furniture layouts to providing flooring and wall covering selections.

George and Judy Reimer still own the majority interest, but Judy left the day-to-day operations in the early 1990s to pursue a master of divinity degree. George remained in the operations area until September of 1998. The current management team at Harris consists of Doug Hyre and the Reimers' son, Troy, both of whom are principals in the company.

Harris Office's staff is an integral part of the success of the company. The company's strong team atmosphere is reflected in the longevity in employment of its staff. In addition, Harris Office continues to emphasize customer service. Although the company serves the entire state, its concentration is within 100 miles of Roanoke.

The Harris "full service" concept means that the customer is taken care of every step of the way. From the professional sales staff to the designers, support staff, and installation, Harris meets individual needs with efficiency and cost-effectiveness. Long-standing relationships with premier manufacturers such as Herman Miller and Hon have helped maintain the reputation of the company.

As it continues to meet the needs of the changing business community, the focus of the Harris Office team remains the customer. Harris Office has developed into a leader in innovative office environments and will continue to furnish spaces with quality new and used office furniture. ■

PHOTOGRAPHY COURTESY OF HERMAN MILLER INC. PHOTOGRAPHER: NICK MERRICK. HEDRICH-BLESSING.

12

CHAPTER

TWELVE

REAL ESTATE,
DEVELOPMENT, AND
CONSTRUCTION

PHOTO BY DOUG MILLER.

LANFORD BROTHERS COMPANY, INC.

BRIDGE DECK OVERLAY
BEING PLACED.

Although most travelers are not excited about road-repair projects, bridge repair is actually a very sophisticated technology. Lanford Brothers Company, Inc., of Roanoke, prides itself on being one of the leaders in this field.

Lanford Brothers is also involved in bridge and box culvert construction, as well as having specialty operations, such as milling concrete and asphalt, grooving and shotblasting, and latex concrete operations.

In the 40 years since its incorporation, the company has built more than 700 projects with an average year's volume exceeding $12 million. In recent years, Lanford forces have repaired more than 200 bridges each year.

The company has projects over a four-state area: Virginia, North Carolina, West Virginia, and South Carolina. While much of its work is in high traffic areas—such as Interstate 81—there are some local projects—such as Explore Park—in the Roanoke area.

Lanford Brothers Company has been a pioneer in new methods, machinery, and technologies of concrete and road building and repair. The company was one of the first to invest in milling machines, the equipment that removes old asphalt from bridges and roads without jackhammers. It was the first to use shotblasting equipment to replace sand-blasting for cleaning and repairing concrete surfaces, as well.

Shotblasters use steel shot instead of silica sand, cutting down on dust and making operations safer for employees. Lanford also pioneered the use of latex mobiles, which are used to place latex modified concrete overlays, which protect the concrete deck from salt damage and traffic.

When a job must be finished quickly, Lanford Brothers uses epoxy overlays, which can reduce the time the bridge is not in service. Other areas Lanford Brothers has branched into include latex slurry, steel repair, cathodic protection, and bridge jacking.

As its name suggests, Lanford Brothers is a family business with roots going back to the road-building days following World War I. S.F. Lanford Sr. bought out part of his uncle's road-building business and carried on the tradition with a partner, expanding into excavation work. He brought in his sons after their respective graduations (Jack, Virginia Military Institute, 1953; Stan, University of Virginia, 1955) and they ran the company after his death in 1955.

LANFORD BROTHERS,
MILLING DIVISION,
EQUIPMENT AND SUPERVISORS.

In 1960, the brothers decided to concentrate on bridge and concrete structures and incorporated the company as Lanford Brothers Company. Today, Stan oversees the operations at Lanford and Jack handles Adams Construction Company, the paving company in which they have an interest.

The next generation of Lanfords, as well as several field superintendent's relations, are now active in the operation. Three of Stan's four children work for the company. The management team, which includes these offspring and several others with many years' experience, keep the office running.

However, everyone knows the actual construction occurs in the field. Lanford Brothers' greatest strength is the people who work for the company. Many who came to Lanford as young people have decided to stay for their careers. Lanford Brothers also has several second-generation supervisors who worked for their fathers at Lanford Brothers and now carry on their own family traditions. A lot of repeat business is generated because of the desire Lanford crews have to get the job done right the first time.

In 1984, the company went to an Employee Stock Ownership Plan (ESOP) to promote the idea that employees should work their entire careers at Lanford Brothers and have a hand in building their retirement funds.

The ESOP has been successful, with 100 employees owning 85 percent of the company. The ESOP has more benefits than originally figured. The workforce turnover went from 500 W2s in 1986 to 250 in recent years, with the volume of work increasing.

The company uses bonuses and earnings distributions to remind younger employees who do not think of retiring any time soon of the value of owning stock. As the company makes a profit, it is shared with the employees who make it possible in other ways, such as with ESOP contributions, safety prizes, and a Christmas party for employees and their families.

As employees work hard, work safely, and work smarter, they have seen the value of the ESOP stock increase. As the value of stock and years of service increase, employees see their ESOP accounts increase and they care. They care about their jobs, and therefore, do a better job for Lanford Brothers Company and for the customers who pay to have the work done.

Lanford Brothers Company has built a solid reputation for reliability and efficiency. The years of experience and successfully operating makes it the top choice for highway rehabilitation and heavy construction. Lanford provides services for a variety of clients, such as the Virginia Department of Transportation, North Carolina and South Carolina Departments of Transportation, West Virginia Department of Transportation, U.S. Army Corps of Engineers, U.S. Navy, and various cities, counties, and turnpike authorities.

Lanford Brothers' goal is to meet or exceed the demands of the customer. It prides itself on providing its customers with safe, quality jobs on schedule. Stan Lanford explains: "One job leads to another with satisfied customers. We help our customers with their problems and meet their deadlines and budgetary restrictions and, in turn, this helps us grow. We believe we are strongly positioned to meet the needs of our clients well into the future."

Lanford Brothers Company takes pride in being part of the Roanoke Valley business community and is committed to working with local governments and other businesses to continually improve the quality of life in the Valley. ∎

FIFTH STREET BRIDGE ABUTMENT BEING FORMED IN ROANOKE, VIRGINIA.

SHOTBLASTER CLEANING A BRIDGE DECK.

THE BRANCH GROUP, INC.

MAINTAINING A TRADITION OF EXCELLENCE

The Branch Group, Inc., has been a driving force in the economic development of the Roanoke Valley for over 35 years. Founded by Billy Branch in 1963, and now a 100-percent employee-owned (ESOP) construction company headquartered in Roanoke, Virginia, The Branch Group has experienced tremendous growth. Now one of the largest employers in the Roanoke Valley, and ranked the 168th largest construction company in the country, the Branch Group serves the valley with three sub-sidiaries: Branch & Associates, Inc., Branch Highways, Inc., and G. J. Hopkins, Inc.

BRANCH & ASSOCIATES, INC.

Branch & Associates, Inc., the commercial construction arm of The Branch Group, provides general contracting, design-build, and construction management services through-out Virginia, West Virginia, North Carolina, and Tennessee. Now the largest building contractor based in Southwest Virginia, the company is financially solid, maintaining a bonding capacity in excess of $250 million with a $50 million per project aggregate.

The Branch team is comprised of a highly skilled group of pre-construction professionals, construction management teams, field operation supervisors, and skilled constructors. According to Stephen Cirbee, Branch & Associates director of Business Development, the company has achieved its strong position in the business because of an unblemished reputation and an ability to perform in various market sec-tors of the construction industry, while remaining competitive on cost. Branch's diverse markets include light and heavy industrial projects, educational facilities, multi-family apartment and condominium buildings, the health-care and hospitality markets, and state and municipal government projects, such as courthouses and detention centers.

"Branch typically focuses its attention towards the larger more challenging projects in the region, as well as highly complex and technical work. We also specialize in 'fast track' construction projects," says Cirbee. "We are able to provide businesses in this area, and also new businesses relocating to this area, the option of utilizing a local contractor for their large complex projects. There is no need to bring in a large national firm. We have the ability to handle any project that the economy of this region can sustain."

In recent years, Branch has expanded its ability to provide alternative project delivery methods such as design-build and construction management, in addition to the typical design-bid-build and negotiated general contracting approaches. Recent accomplishments utilizing these methods include Echo Star Communications, an $8.2 million call center, designed and built under a design-build contract in less than six months. The Sweet Briar College Campus Center is another, with Branch acting as the construction manager for the college's current $13 million building program.

With an unwavering focus on client satisfaction and quality construction, Branch & Associates, Inc., maintains an exemplary record of performance and timely completion of its projects. With a commitment to excellence, Branch & Associates, Inc., strives to achieve the highest standards of performance and management of construction, in a cost-efficient, safe, and timely manner.

BRANCH HIGHWAYS, INC.

Branch Highways, Inc., provides full-service industrial and commercial site grading and development and heavy highway infrastructure construction.

Branch Highways' goal is to meet or exceed the cus-tomer's expectations of quality, scheduling, and investment in preparing their sites for building construction. With over 500 employee-owners including engineers, experienced operators, and highly skilled craftsmen, Branch Highways maintains a capital investment in heavy equipment in excess of $35 million.

Branch Highways is the contractor of choice in Virginia and has the experienced and certified personnel required for tackling the most environmentally demanding jobs. Not only are client's projects kept on schedule, but also well within regulatory guidelines.

Branch Highways' customers return time and time again when critical schedules allow no delay. Branch is called upon by the auto, paper, and retail distribution industries to develop large acreage sites for quick turn around occupation

by moving millions of cubic yards of dirt and rock, installing miles of drainage pipe and grading acres of building pads. Branch's people have known the meaning of the term 24/7 long before it became a buzzword.

"We are continually cognizant of the fact that site preparation can determine the schedule of the entire project…it is the owner's greatest unknown," says Michael Branch, vice president of Business Development. "Through meticulous planning and project management, and dedicated resources, we keep the project on schedule."

Specializing in preparing a site for building, Branch Highways, Inc., has made a positive mark on the landscape of the Roanoke Valley.

G. J. HOPKINS, INC.

Already one of Virginia's largest mechanical/electrical/ service contractors with over 40 years of experience in new construction and renovation projects, G. J. Hopkins, Inc., enters the new millennium with a renewed commitment to customer satisfaction by building quality products safely and on time. Featuring a dedicated staff of mechanical, electrical, and technology specialists, G. J. Hopkins has long been recognized as the industry leader, providing its clients with a single source for complete systems integration and design/build services.

The advancements and demands of the IT environment have created new challenges in the construction market and G. J. Hopkins, Inc., has responded by offering a full spectrum of high-tech services for building automated systems, data/communications networks, and industrial process controls. G. J. Hopkins' emphasis on the continuing education and training of its field personnel provides its customers with a variety of industry certified mechanics, experienced in performing quality installations and service in the fields of fiber-optic wiring, pneumatics, PLC controllers, and category six cabling.

G. J. Hopkins has a deep résumé of successfully completed projects involving health-care facilities in the Roanoke Valley region. The Hopkins team includes technicians who have passed a rigorous examination for licensure as medical gas piping experts, insuring that hospital and laboratory clients will comply with the required standards

necessary to meet state and federal certifications. Engineering support, a wealth of historic cost information, and the experience to minimize shutdowns gives G. J. Hopkins the ability to provide the medical community with an array of services to guide them through the complexities of additions and renovations to their facilities.

Hospitals, factories, and commercial businesses have come to rely on the 24/7 mechanical/electrical/communication repair capabilities offered by the Hopkins service department. Quick response and the ability to handle catastrophic situations, like the electrical fire that destroyed the main switchboard at a local hospital, has made G. J. Hopkins the region's choice for fast, dependable service. As Charlie Smith, director of Engineering and Maintenance for Carilion Roanoke Community Hospital said, "It was an outstanding effort to completely remove and replace the main switch gear in two and a half weeks. If it had not been for G. J. Hopkins, our hospital would have been shut down for a much longer time."

Unequalled service, continuing education, and pride of ownership drives the employees of G. J. Hopkins, Inc., toward their long-held mission, to be the preferred mechanical/electrical/service contractor by providing quality service to its customers and community.

THE BRANCH GROUP GIVES BACK TO THE COMMUNITY

In addition to providing the highest level of service to businesses in the Roanoke Valley, The Branch Group, Inc., maintains a policy of giving back to the community through such organizations as Habitat for Humanity, the United Way, and the Bikes or Bust program for underprivileged children. The Branch Group, Inc., also participates in the underwriting of various public television programs. In keeping with a tradition of excellence and a philosophy of giving back, The Branch Group stays involved in community projects, believing that doing so benefits everyone. ■

13

CHAPTER THIRTEEN

HEALTH CARE, EDUCATION, AND QUALITY OF LIFE

PHOTO BY DOUG MILLER.

ROANOKE COUNTY

Roanoke County encompasses 240 square miles in Southwest Virginia, surrounding the cities of Roanoke and Salem. The county prides itself on the physical beauty of the area, the quality of life provided to its citizens, excellent human services, and an emphasis on cultural enrichment that spans the generations.

Newcomers are continually attracted to Roanoke County with its strong, stable economy and its enthusiastic spirit, as well as the conveniences and opportunities of a big city, and its exceptional natural beauty. The area offers a diversity of lifestyles, ranging from rural to suburban to urban.

Roanoke County has been a leader among local governments in the state. It was the second county to be granted a charter by the General Assembly, and the first in Virginia to be named an All-America City. The police department was one of the first in the region to be nationally accredited, and Spring Hollow Reservoir boasts the largest dam of its type on the East Coast.

The state-of-the-art waste management system is regional, with a transfer station in the city of Roanoke, and a landfill at Smith Gap in Roanoke County, linked by Norfolk Southern's Waste Line Express train. Other regional projects include the Roanoke Regional Airport, a new juvenile detention center, the fire and rescue training center, the wastewater treatment plant, and a cooperative library system.

Roanoke County citizens participated in a visioning process in 1995, which was used to create a new comprehensive plan for the future. The citizens placed importance on maintaining the quality of life, encouraging a regional approach to services, sustaining the natural resources of the area, preserving the identity of the community, and retaining the scenic beauty of the Roanoke Valley. The vision report placed an emphasis on education, economic development, and appropriate land use to help Roanoke County achieve these goals.

The Board of Supervisors has taken these suggestions and used them in planning for the future. There is a continued focus on the quality of education to help provide a skilled workforce and high-quality employees. Workforce development is elementary in attracting the type of industry Roanoke County wants for the future.

Countywide planning involving appropriate land use, economic development, transportation, and protection of the environment also remains a focal point. The county recognizes the fragile balance between economic growth and prosperity while maintaining the beauty and integrity of the region.

This commitment is evidenced at the Center for Research and Technology (CRT), a 457-acre business park in western Roanoke County. It is a place of compelling beauty and extraordinary opportunity. Here technology and talent thrive.

The center features state-of-the-art infrastructure and well-crafted covenants and architectural controls. Amenities include pathways and picnic tables, rolling hills, and Blue Ridge Mountain vistas.

The Roanoke Valley is the transportation and shipping center of Southwest Virginia and CRT is at the heart of things, adjacent to Interstate 81, while the regional airport is 15 minutes away and provides ready access to the nation's airline hubs.

The county also supports cultural enrichment and recreational programs, both through its own departments, and through financial contributions to arts groups and facilities. Soccer and Little League baseball are favorite sports for children and several tournaments are played each year at the county's larger facilities.

The Teen Center, the Senior Citizens program, and the Leisure Arts Center are located at the Brambleton Center, providing a new life for a former school building (which once served as the County Administration Building, as well).

Virginia's Explore Park, a living history facility along the Blue Ridge Parkway, provides a glimpse of life along the Virginia frontier during the middle of the 19th century, while Center in the Square (with its seven attractions), the Mill Mountain Zoo, and the Virginia Museum of Transportation contribute other facets to the lives of county residents. The Blue Ridge Parkway and Appalachian Trail provide plentiful outdoor recreational opportunities for residents and visitors alike.

Life in Roanoke County remains a blend of the old and new. The citizens have put a priority on maintaining a people-friendly environment, while providing a supportive atmosphere for new and existing business. ■

THE ROANOKE COUNTY BOARD OF SUPERVISORS MEETS TWICE MONTHLY TO SET POLICY FOR COUNTY OPERATION. PICTURED, FROM LEFT: BOB L. JOHNSON, H. ODELL "FUZZY" MINNIX, JOSEPH P. MCNAMARA, JOE B. "BUTCH" CHURCH, AND HARRY C. NICKENS.

PART OF THE Y2K CELEBRATION INCLUDED A BALLOON FESTIVAL AT ROANOKE COUNTY'S GREEN HILL PARK.

ROANOKE COUNTY SCHOOLS

SYNERGISTIC LAB TECHNOLOGY OFFERS EXCEPTIONAL LEARNING OPPORTUNITIES.

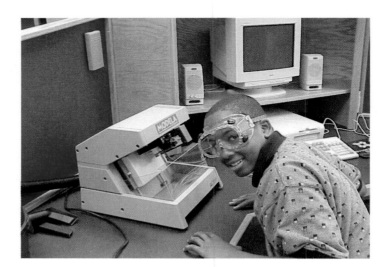

A cademic achievement, community involvement, technology, and emphasis on the arts are all part of the strengths of the Roanoke County school system. With an enrollment of approximately 13,900 students, Roanoke County is the area's largest school system and continues to receive widespread recognition for academic excellence. It ranks among the state's top school divisions in both reading and math achievement, with 86 percent of 2000 graduates going on to higher education. The division has the largest dual-enrollment/college credit program in the area. SAT scores exceed the state and national averages in both verbal and math. Students in Roanoke County continue to demonstrate progress in achieving the goals established by the Virginia Board of Education outlined in The Standards of Accrediting Public Schools in Virginia. Of the 28 tests administered, student performance between 1999 and 2000 increased on 20 tests.

Roanoke County offers a traditional course of study, system-wide technological opportunities, and a wide range of gifted, special education, and career and technical programs. Emphasis continues to be placed on reading, phonics, writing, mathematics, and scientific skills beginning in kindergarten and continuing through high school. Technology is also emphasized in the learning process, with instructors using computers for mathematics, experiments with scientific formulas, and simulated travel and business experiences. The curriculum is designed to meet the varied needs of the students. The diversity of subjects offered enables students to make choices designed to prepare them for further education after high school or for a vocation. Within each area of the curriculum, programs are specifically designed to enhance classroom instruction and contribute to the overall education and well being of each student.

ROANOKE COUNTY SCHOOLS OFFERS QUALITY LEARNING EXPERIENCES THAT ENABLE STUDENTS TO GROW, ADAPT, AND MEET THE CHALLENGES OF A CHANGING WORLD.

A formal local school-based program is available for gifted and talented students in kindergarten through grade 12 whose mental development is accelerated to the extent that the student can advance to specifically planned educational opportunities different from those provided by the general program.

Additionally, extensive career and technical programs that stress both academic and practical application are offered in all secondary schools. Programs are available in business, marketing, work and family studies, technology, trade and industrial occupations, health professions, and horticulture. In addition, Arnold R. Burton Technology Center offers a variety of vocational and technical classes that prepare students for the workforce and for further education.

The Roanoke County School System is composed of 17 elementary schools, 5 middle schools, 4 high schools, 1 career and technical center, and 2 alternative education centers. All schools are accredited by the State Board of Education, with elementary and high schools accredited or affiliated with the Southern Association of Colleges and Schools.

Appointed by the Roanoke County School Board, the chief executive officer of the Roanoke County School System is the superintendent. Under the superintendent are the deputy superintendent, two assistant superintendents, and directors in the areas of special education, technology, career and technical education, and adult education. Serving under the directors are supervisors of instructional services, administrative services, federal programs, and support services.

The Roanoke County School System's commitment to staff development has resulted in an outstanding organization of school administrators, instructors, guidance counselors, and support personnel dedicated to providing students with the knowledge and skills needed to achieve success.

The strong PTA programs in each school provide varied volunteer opportunities for parents to assist during the school day, as well as outside school hours. Parent advisory committees and

program is available to both youth and adults in the Roanoke Valley. Programs offered include: GED and SAT Review, English as a Second Language, Nursing Assistant Licensing, personal use and enrichment courses, various computer classes, and all occupational related courses.

The new millennium was marked with important changes, including a new elementary school opening in Bonsack and major renovations at Clearbrook and Burlington Elementary Schools and in the science labs at the secondary schools. Additionally, construction began on Hidden Valley High School, a new high school in South Roanoke County.

The Open Doors Open Minds: Accessible Schools for All established independent access to school buildings for disabled students, and business-school partnerships enable schools and the community to work together for mutual benefit.

other programs are in effect in all schools, allowing parents the opportunity to actively participate in the students' education. This parent participation is highly encouraged by all schools, thereby providing a school/home continuum.

Partnerships are also formed between schools and local businesses. These partnerships enhance the educational program for the students while building bridges between the community and the school system. The Roanoke County School System adheres to the belief that if students are to successfully meet the challenges of today's complex world and become successful contributing adults, then this comprehensive education must be shared.

As Virginia's second largest adult education provider, Roanoke County Schools serves more than 10,000 people annually with adult courses through a business-focused in-house training program, 36 conferences, and 5 teleconferences in conjunction with the Virginia Community College Systems and the Virginia Department of Education. A comprehensive year-round adult- and continuing-education

Roanoke County students have proved themselves in the Commonwealth and in the nation: 2000 Roanoke County graduates received more than $4.8 million in scholarships and 43 students graduated with 4.0 or better averages. Students were accepted at elite colleges and universities throughout the country.

The school system is enthusiastically approaching the cutting edge of technology and its students become increasingly networked with each other and with a world whose boundaries are growing closer. Roanoke County students are stepping up to the challenge in academics, athletics, and the arts in the state, the region, and the nation. Collaborative efforts in the community and business sector, combined with outstanding test scores, innovative teaching initiatives, and student programs are earning students recognition, as the Roanoke County School System continue to strengthen its place within the Commonwealth. ■

SALEM VETERANS AFFAIRS MEDICAL CENTER

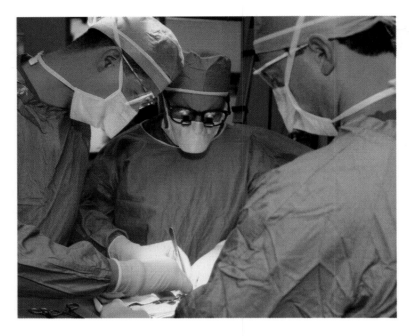

The picturesque Salem Veterans Affairs Medical Center is surrounded by the Blue Ridge and Alleghany Mountains at the southern end of the Shenandoah Valley and is thought of as one of the most modern health-care facilities in the region.

The facility, which is part of the Mid-Atlantic Health Care Network covering Virginia, southeast West Virginia, and North Carolina, offers United States military veterans state-of-the-art medical technology, clinical services, and research programs. The Medical Center's "patients come first" mission is reflected in both the comfortable surroundings and in the way the veterans are treated with dignity and compassion. The Medical Center staff strives to fulfill the physical, psychological, and personal needs of each patient by using available resources in a timely, caring, and cost-effective manner. The Medical Center works closely in partnerships with the surrounding communities and other Roanoke Valley medical facilities.

The Salem Veterans Affairs Medical Center (VAMC) is a 165-bed, general medical-, surgical-, and psychiatric-care facility, complemented by a 90-bed Extended-Care Rehabilitation Center. The medical, surgical, and rehabilitation programs support treatment to veterans living throughout Southwest Virginia while it serves Virginia and West Virginia as a tertiary referral center for acute and long-term psychiatric care.

A comprehensive array of specialized services is provided, including cardiac catheterization, peripheral angioplasty, urology, ophthalmology, orthopedics, CT scanning, cancer treatment, dialysis, nuclear medicine, mental-health clinic, post-traumatic-stress-disorder unit, intensive-care unit, geriatric-evaluation-management unit, substance-abuse residential rehabilitation unit, respite care, sleep-disorder evaluation, veterans outreach, and a day-treatment center.

In addition to these programs, a vibrant Women's Veterans Health Program (GYN clinic), prevention and risk assessment clinic, telemedicine consultative care, comprehensive AIDS/HIV care, spinal-cord-injury outpatient care, blind rehabilitation clinic, homeless veterans treatment, and assistance and preservation amputation care and treatment clinic are provided for veteran patients.

Nine primary care teams, including one for mental health, specialty clinics, and two fee-based group practices in the Tazewell and Danville/Axton areas of Virginia provide ongoing continuity of care for patients.

The extended-care program encompasses the 90-bed Extended Care Rehabilitation Center and a geriatric-evaluation-management unit. Formalized sharing agreements are maintained with local health-care facilities for radiation therapy and MRI.

At the turn of the millennium, Salem VAMC is the 10th largest employer in the Roanoke Valley. In coordination with Carilion Health System, it is affiliated with the University of Virginia School of Medicine for the training of residents and medical students in medical specialties. In addition, associated health training programs are offered in affiliation with 54 other colleges and universities. With a focus on local procurement, the center's commitment to enrich the community is evidenced in the contribution to Western Virginia's economic stability each year, estimated to be in excess of $100 million.

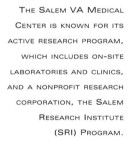

The center is also known for its active research program, which includes an on-site Salem Research Institute (SRI) Program. This program is a nonprofit research corporation established by Salem VA Medical Center personnel to facilitate and administer non-VA appropriated research conducted by VA employees in the facility's laboratories and clinics.

The Salem VAMC is located on 210 acres in Salem. The facility, which was among the first VAMC's, was originally constructed in 1933 on a rural site midway between the City of Roanoke and the Town of Salem, which, at the time, was the county seat of Roanoke County. On October 19, 1934, Clifton A. Woodrum, then representative of the 6th Congressional District, presided at the dedication ceremony and introduced President Franklin Delano Roosevelt. The dedication was a major event in the history of the Roanoke Valley, attracting in excess of 40,000 people, and giving the Salem VA Medical Center the distinction of being the only VAMC to date to be dedicated by a United States President.

Because Roanoke was the larger locality, the facility was initially named the Roanoke Veterans Administration Hospital. In 1960, however, the hospital was annexed by the expanding town of Salem (later to become an independent city) and its name was subsequently changed to the Salem Veterans Affairs Medical Center. In 1960, the Salem VAMC was designated a historic district by the U.S. Secretary of the Interior.

The center is well-known for its dedicated staff of more than 1,300 people providing treatment for more than 5,000 inpatient hospitalizations and 220,000 outpatient visits annually. The VAMC is also known for its team of over 1,000 volunteers contributing their time to assist patients on a daily basis.

The center recently renovated its fitness center, located on the ground level of the main clinical building. The Fitness and Wellness Center features up-to-date fitness equipment, cardiovascular machines, free weights, a basketball court, and other fitness-oriented amenities for both patients and staff.

Additionally, an on-site childcare center for children six weeks old to kindergarten age is operated by Greenvale Nursery School and the Adult Day-Care Center of Roanoke Valley operates an on-site adult day-care program.

Stephen L. Lemons, director of the Salem VAMC, says, "We are very involved with providing health education and comprehensive health care to our patients and to our community. We are extremely interested in improving the quality of life in our region, and we strive to respond quickly to the support needs of our patients, as well as to the needs of the community." ∎

CARILION HEALTH SYSTEM

A not-for-profit organization, Carilion Health System traces its roots to 1899, when the Roanoke Hospital Association built a hospital at the base of Mill Mountain to take care of the sick and injured. The ensuing century of caring has been made possible by community involvement and commitment, a dedicated, caring staff and physicians, specialized services, and top-notch hospitals and medical clinics.

Today, Carilion operates 11 community hospitals, including Burrell Nursing Center, Carilion Bedford

Memorial Hospital, Carilion Franklin Memorial Hospital, Carilion Giles Memorial Hospital, Carilion New River Valley Medical Center, Carilion Roanoke Community Hospital, Carilion Roanoke Memorial Hospital, Carilion Saint Albans Hospital, Smyth County Community Hospital, Tazewell Community Hospital, and Wythe County Community Hospital. With over 160 physician members, Carilion offers one of the largest primary-care groups in Virginia, encompassing practices from Galax to Woodstock. And, Carilion Health Plans is the first and only locally owned and developed health plan for employers throughout western Virginia.

Regardless of its growth, Carilion still honors its original mission: to improve the health of the communities it serves by assuring accessible, affordable, quality health care that meets the needs of the community. One of the most effective ways that the system makes good on its mission is by forming mutually beneficial partnerships with various organizations—both medical and non-medical—within the community. The Carilion Community Health Fund (CCHF) provides grants to programs that show broad community commitment through matching funds and in-kind services. These projects combine the resources of health and human service organizations, schools, Public Health Departments, the business sector, local governments, and churches. Since the fund's inception in 1997, Carilion has given approximately $6 million to assist these community endeavors.

CARILION ROANOKE MEMORIAL HOSPITAL PERFORMS OVER 1,200 OPEN HEART SURGERIES AND 6,000 CARDIAC CATHETERIZATIONS EACH YEAR.

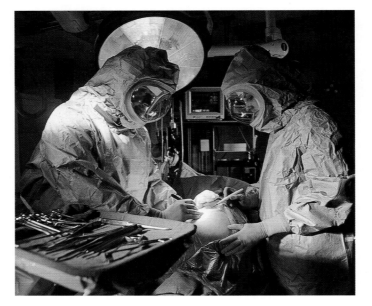

WITH THE SUPPORT OF BOTH AIR AND GROUND TRANSPORTATION SERVICES, CARILION ROANOKE MEMORIAL HOSPITAL OPERATES ONE OF THE FIVE LEVEL ONE TRAUMA CENTERS IN VIRGINIA.

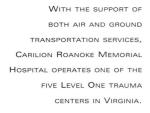

Developing a range of specialized services is a critical part of being a fully integrated system. In that field, Carilion is a leader with a long and diverse track record. For example, in conjunction with the University of Virginia, Carilion provides an extensive medical education program to train future physicians. Residencies include general surgery, family practice, OB/GYN, internal medicine, orthopedics, and psychiatry. As a result, Carilion brings the latest medical knowledge into the region and serves as a major source for providing new physicians.

Carilion also provides the only Level One Trauma Center in western Virginia at Carilion Roanoke Memorial Hospital. Here, they treat the most serious illnesses and have surgeons and anesthesiologists available around the clock. Life-Guard 10, a 24-hour-a-day emergency medical helicopter service, has been an integral part of the trauma center since 1982.

Another key service is the Carilion Medical Center for Children at Roanoke Community Hospital, which provides comprehensive pediatric clinical and support services in such specialized areas as cardiology, oncology, gastroenterology, pulmonology, pediatric surgery, and neonatology. The center is also the regional pediatric referral center for western Virginia and one of more than 150 hospitals affiliated with the Children's Miracle Network.

Recognizing the coming "age wave"—the significant growth in the 65-plus population—Carilion also offers specialized services for the other end of the age spectrum. The new Carilion Center for Healthy Aging brings together geriatric experts in one site to provide comprehensive assessments and education. The center is unique in this part of the state and serves as a consultative resource to older people, families, and health-care providers. Carilion also offers the Viva senior membership program to help people stay healthy and more fully enjoy the second half of life.

Carilion Roanoke Memorial Hospital (CRMH) has been a leader in cardiac care in the region for over 30 years. It was the first hospital in the region to perform cardiac catheterizations. Since 1998, CRMH has been one of just 100 medical

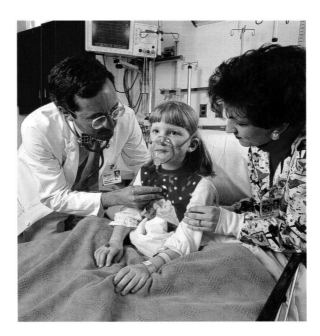

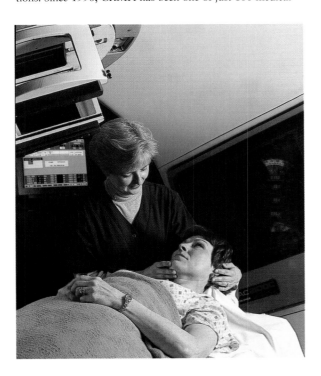

centers in the U.S. to offer an alternative to traditional open heart surgery called Port-Access—a minimally-invasive procedure that allows patients to recover faster. CRMH is an award-winning cardiovascular hospital—*U.S. News and World Report* listed it among the top 50 hospitals in heart surgery in their 1999 10th Annual Guide to America's Best Hospitals.

The system has also been honored in other areas of patient treatment. In 2000, the HCIA-Sachs Institute jointly named CRMH and Carilion Roanoke Community Hospital to the 100 Top Hospitals list for orthopedic and stroke care.

Carilion has been on the leading edge of cancer care as tremendous strides have been made in the treatment of cancer nationally. It established strong affiliations with major research centers, bringing the latest, most promising clinical research trials to patients. Since 1975, more than 500 patients have been given the opportunity to receive investigational treatments without traveling outside the area. The Carilion Cancer Center of Western Virginia was dedicated in 1980 and gained a nationwide reputation. The center was accredited in 1994 as a "Community Hospital Comprehensive Cancer Program," which is one of the highest designations a hospital can attain. Today, the Cancer Center has more physician cancer specialists than any other facility in western Virginia.

Given the strong belief in cooperative ventures, it is not surprising that Carilion has grown and broadened its capabilities through various strategic affiliations and partnerships over the years. One of the newest and possibly most innovative is the Carilion Biomedical Institute (please refer to the section on the Institute located in this book).

Carilion certainly shares in the Star City's reputation in southwest Virginia by being a beacon of light, showing the way to excellence in health care close to home. For more than a century, the community has turned to Carilion for their health-care needs and Carilion has tracked its success by one golden standard—the ability to improve the health and well-being of the community it serves. Carilion has met its challenge through fresh and innovative programs throughout the past century and plans to continue providing its patients with the best possible care in the future. ■

THE CARILION MEDICAL CENTER FOR CHILDREN AT ROANOKE COMMUNITY HOSPITAL IS DEDICATED TO PROTECTING AND PRESERVING HEALTHY LIFESTYLES IN CHILDREN FROM BIRTH TO ADOLESCENCE.

THE CARILION CANCER CENTER OF WESTERN VIRGINIA COMBINES THE LATEST MEDICAL SKILLS WITH THE NEWEST TECHNOLOGIES TO HELP DETECT, FIGHT, AND SURVIVE CANCER.

NORTH CROSS SCHOOL

N orth Cross School, the only independent, non-sectarian, college-preparatory school in the Roanoke Valley, was founded in 1960 through the merger of The Northcross School of Salem, The Eaton School of Roanoke County, and The Wellington School of Roanoke City to promote accelerated learning and character development. North Cross School has a vision of education that integrates knowledge and character, and asserts that strong values significantly define the individual. The School has a reputation for producing graduates who matriculate at the nation's most prestigious colleges and universities and who have a positive impact on their communities.

A dedicated, well-educated faculty, serving as mentors and leaders as well as teachers, facilitates learning, both in the classroom and on the field or stage. They breathe life into the subjects they teach and are committed to the process of exploration and discovery that motivates students to excel. Faculty members form personal bonds with students and families, sponsoring extra-curricular activities from sports teams and school publications to music and drama performances.

North Cross School, situated on a 77-acre campus in southwest Roanoke County, serves 550 children from age four through graduation. Committed to providing a quality education to students showing academic ability and promise, the School distributes over $250,000 in need-based financial assistance as well as merit scholarships. Its growing facilities include three academic buildings, a fine arts center, a stunning athletic facility, and an administrative building, which houses the extensive library collection.

The Lower School is committed to providing an exceptional academic program in a personalized, nurturing environment. The goal of the teachers is to focus on the individual talents and abilities of each child, ensuring that their learning experience will be both challenging and successful. The well-balanced curriculum includes P.E., music, art, and Spanish beginning in Junior Kindergarten.

The Middle School is tailored to the unique needs of early adolescent students who are undergoing rapid intellectual, physical, and social growth. While the curriculum is rooted in basic scholastic ideals, teachers explore creative ways of pursuing education in an atmosphere where students experience the exhilaration of learning.

The Upper School promotes increasing independence while remaining mindful of the need for individualized support as students discover their academic potential. Within the liberal arts program, students explore academic and personal interests as they prepare for the rigors of college. Critical thinking, scientific inquiry, artistic expression, and technical literacy are emphasized, along with the development of written and oral communication. Each year 100 percent of the seniors are accepted for post-secondary education.

Values—including respect for others and uncompromising honesty—lie at the heart of a North Cross education, and the Honor System is an integral part of campus life. Because North Cross strongly encourages the development of character as well as intellect, all students participate in community service projects.

North Cross fosters learning, self-discovery, and personal accountability in the pursuit of knowledge, and strives to instill in each student a broadened perspective, while nourishing clarity of thought, facility of expression, and competence in critical thinking. Although graduates are expected to excel in national colleges and universities, the School's highest purpose is to create a challenging but charitable environment, where students gain the skills and strengths necessary for a meaningful and rewarding life. ■

ROANOKE HIGHER EDUCATION CENTER

T he Roanoke skyline, looking west from I-581, has a brighter nighttime look. The windows of the Roanoke Higher Education Center glitter with lights illuminating evening classes.

The newly renovated building, formerly headquarters of the Norfolk & Western Railway, one of the largest employers in the region during the industrial age, houses the dynamic new downtown Center that provides leadership in education and training for the information age.

New life for the building means new opportunity for the people of the region, as 16 agencies and institutions deliver training and education to meet the ever-widening array of needs that will continue to grow as the region broadens its economic base.

Students from high school age through retirement age are able to find programs that give them a career start, a career boost, or a change in career direction. Whether through short-term training, retraining, or the more lengthy pursuit of an advanced degree, students have an opportunity to broaden their knowledge, skills, and interests in ways that enrich their lives and the overall quality of life in the region.

Guided by community needs and interests, advice from business and civic leaders and the experience of member institutions, programs make education in Virginia's largest metropolitan area without a four-year public institution more accessible than has been possible in the past.

Distance learning technology plays an important role in the collaborative efforts that characterize many of the educational offerings. The Center allows for an exceptionally broad set of educational opportunities including industrial technology, medical services, culinary arts, and business for high school students; job training and retraining for adults; and career guidance for both. Additionally, the Center provides opportunities to pursue undergraduate degrees in a variety of disciplines and fields related to regional job openings. Graduate degree programs are also available in support of further career development and in preparation for social and technological change. The Center's design

creates an environment that encourages lifelong education and training.

The Center is part of the larger effort to stimulate economic development in the region, while it is also a cornerstone in the revitalization of the historic Gainsboro neighborhood.

The synergy of regional economic development and downtown Roanoke redevelopment efforts generates training and educational opportunity for people at all levels of educational need. The Center is a multidimensional project that produces a substantial positive impact in the region as a whole, and provides the Commonwealth and the nation with a new model for collaboration in training and education.

The Roanoke Higher Education Center is unique in the number and kind of organizations collaborating to expand educational access. Partners in the new center include Averett College, Bluefield College, Blue Ridge Technical Academy, College of Health Sciences, Ferrum College, Fifth District Employment and Training Consortium, Hampton University, Hollins University, Mary Baldwin College, Old Dominion University, Radford University, Roanoke College, Total Action Against Poverty's (TAP) This Valley Works, University of Virginia, Virginia Tech, and Virginia Western Community College.

The center is designed to incorporate state-of-the-art instructional, communication, and computer technology that supports distance learning, as well as on-site instruction. Other features important to students, particularly working adults, include a childcare center, a café, and a technologically advanced library.

The public and private investment in the center is already achieving a powerful yield for the advancement of workforce training, higher education, and the further development of the Roanoke Valley and Virginia's Technology Corridor. Additional information on the center is available at its Web site, www.education.edu. ■

LEFT: THE CENTER'S SPECTACULAR LOBBY JUXTAPOSES THE ART DECO FEEL OF THE '30S WITH HIGH-TECH TOUCH-SCREEN DIRECTORIES OF THE 21ST CENTURY. THROUGH THE DIRECTORIES STUDENTS CAN FIND COURSE LISTINGS, LOCATIONS, FLOOR PLANS, STAFF DIRECTORIES, AND LINKS TO MEMBER ORGANIZATIONS' WEB PAGES.

BELOW: THE CENTER'S WEST ENTRANCE AT DUSK, AFTER A FULL DAY OF CLASSES, SEMINARS, AND MEETINGS, LIGHTING UP FOR THE DAILY ROUND OF EVENING CLASSES. THE CENTER IS ALIVE WITH EDUCATIONAL ACTIVITY DURING THE WORKWEEK FROM 8 IN THE MORNING UNTIL 10 AT NIGHT, AND DOESN'T MISS A BEAT UNTIL LATE ON SATURDAY AFTERNOON.

TOWN OF VINTON

TOWN CLOCK.

It's been over 100 years since the farming settlement of Gish's Mill signed a charter that would change its destiny. Today, the Town of Vinton has a unique character, combining urban services and amenities with small-town charm.

Founded in 1884, Vinton comprises 3.2 square miles with a population of approximately 8,000. Its small-town atmosphere is underscored by its low crime rate, moderately priced homes, prosperous businesses, quality schools, responsive public services, an abundance of recreational facilities, and an absence of city congestion.

The Blue Ridge Parkway is immediately east of Vinton, and Explore Park—one of the area's top tourist attractions—is just a short drive up the Parkway. Just beyond the neighboring Bedford County line is Smith Mountain Lake, one of the region's premier water sport and vacation living developments.

The Vinton War Memorial is a flagship municipal center, constructed in 1948 to recognize sacrifices during WWII. The facility is used daily by the public for dinner and community meetings, family celebrations, the annual Vinton Dogwood Festival, and dozens of other occasions.

The Town of Vinton, which has its own council, is part of Roanoke County and is also represented on the County's Board of Supervisors.

Citizens pay real estate and personal property taxes to Roanoke County and the Town of Vinton. Collection of these additional payments allows for enhanced police, fire, rescue, street, planning and zoning, and public works services. The County provides library, health department, social services, parks, and recreation opportunities. Vinton's water and sewer departments provides service to the Town and to eastern Roanoke County.

VINTON WAR MEMORIAL.

Vinton's children attend Roanoke County schools, among the top-performing schools in the state. In addition to several of the County's elementary schools, the community is home to William Byrd Middle School, William Byrd High School, and Roanoke County Career Center.

Vinton and the County recently entered into an innovative "gain share agreement," the first instrument of its specific type in the state, based on the principle that each locality benefits from the other's gains. A particular challenge facing Vinton is that the Town's land is almost completely built out. But while it could annex additional land from the County to meet its growth needs, they have agreed to share in the development of East Roanoke County.

Several years ago, Vinton purchased an open 100-acre tract in the East County for development. Extensive citizen input was sought before going ahead with the project. The plan is to develop the land for economic impact.

As the 20th century becomes the 21st century, Vinton finds itself in a renewal mode. Town Council has launched a new series of community meetings to involve citizens in shaping the Town's future. Town Council has authorized a study of its downtown center and its major corridors.

Vinton may hold steadfast to its small town atmosphere, but the Town is committed to steady progress on the road to the next millennium. ■

OAKEY'S FUNERAL SERVICE & CREMATORY

Since 1866, when John M. Oakey founded Oakey's Funeral Service, the company has helped families through challenging times. During times of grief, Oakey's Funeral Service offers families the services and support needed to achieve peace of mind and closure when saying goodbye to a loved one. By taking care of essential details, Oakey's helps in easing the emotional burden for both family and friends.

Oakey's Funeral Service continues to meet the changing needs of the community with five chapels throughout the Roanoke Valley and a compassionate and experienced staff to offer personalized service.

Oakey's caring staff meets with each family to determine the most appropriate service, timing, and personal touches to preserve memories and celebrate the life of the loved one.

At Oakey's, the staff and owners believe there are no "typical" funeral services or ceremonies. Each family is different and has a special way of remembering the life of a loved one. For this reason, Oakey's offers a variety of ceremonies, from traditional and veterans services to cremation and immediate burial services.

The comfort and personal requests of those Oakey's serves are of paramount importance. The staff will also assist in adding special touches, such as flowers, photographs, and memorial items that capture the essence of the loved one.

Oakey's Funeral Service offers complete pre-need consultations and planning services, from initial conferences with family members to publication of an obituary in newspapers to assistance in obtaining various survivors benefits and after-care services. With more than 100 years of service, the goal remains to offer the most complete and compassionate assistance to the community during times of need.

For generations, Oakey's Funeral Service has not only cared for families in the Roanoke Valley, but has also cared for the community. This is evidenced in the commitment to support numerous charitable organizations, such as Relay for Life, Family Services of the Roanoke Valley, and the Roanoke Wildlife Rescue.

Oakey's is proud to be an integral part of the Roanoke Valley and will continue to provide the best service possible at a reasonable cost, ever mindful that compassion and support remain at the forefront of its mission. ■

SAMMY OAKEY, PRESIDENT, OAKEY'S FUNERAL SERVICE.

OAKEY'S FUNERAL SERVICE & CREMATORY, ROANOKE CHAPEL.

THE GLEBE

Residents, prospective residents, and senior housing professionals overwhelmingly agree that the greatest security, value, and peace of mind for seniors and their families are provided through Full Lifecare retirement communities, such as The Glebe.

Residents of Full Lifecare communities are planners—they want to know that they have planned for whatever their needs may be in the future. The beauty of Full Lifecare is truly realized when residents actually require assistance. As residents' needs change, they will be secure in their knowledge that high-quality, supportive services and care will be available when needed. In addition to peace of mind, residents find private accommodations and an attractive, professional environment at a cost equal to the residential rate in their apartment or cottage and significantly below the market rate for nursing care.

With assisted living, memory support, and nursing care located on site, residents of The Glebe will know that their future needs will be met. In this way, residents may protect their assets from potentially catastrophic health-care costs, and they will be able to predict their living expenses even when health care is needed.

The Glebe is a Full Lifecare retirement community where the joys of a simpler time have been combined with the conveniences of modern-day living—the way a retirement community should be.

There was a time when every neighborhood was safe, when banks, libraries, and restaurants were centrally located, when "a walk in the park" was so enjoyable that the phrase became synonymous with all that is free and easy.

All of this can be found at The Glebe, a Full Lifecare retirement community in the Roanoke Valley. Nestled in the Valley with wonderful mountain views, The Glebe offers everything a retirement community should: superb quality of life, active residents, and convenient living.

A lovely site and beautiful residences are among the reasons The Glebe is the choice of many seniors who have selected the Roanoke Valley as their home. The site for The Glebe is in Daleville, just minutes from downtown Roanoke.

One of four retirement communities operated by Virginia Baptist Homes, The Glebe offers seven spacious apartment floor plans, as well as three cottage home floor plans. The Community Center is designed as the heart of The Glebe and offers a full-service bank, convenience store, formal dining, a bistro, a private dining room, library, woodworking shop, art studio, billiards room, card/game rooms, a wellness center, and much more. Nearby facilities offer a variety of activities from golf to tennis. ∎

THE GLEBE BEGAN ACCEPTING RESERVATIONS IN 1998 AND IS PROJECTED TO OPEN IN LATE 2003.

(ABOVE) STREETSCAPE OF COTTAGES AT THE GLEBE. (RIGHT) A VIEW OF THE GLEBE'S COMMUNITY CENTER.

14

C H A P T E R

F O U R T E E N

Marketplace, Hospitality, and Tourism

Photo by Dan Smith.

WYNDHAM ROANOKE AIRPORT

Professional, caring, and dedicated service are the hallmarks of the Wyndham Roanoke Airport, a hotel for the new century.

Surrounded by the picturesque Blue Ridge Mountains, Wyndham Roanoke Airport is just minutes from downtown Roanoke and directly adjacent to the Roanoke Regional Airport. In August 1999, Wyndham purchased the former Airport Marriott and now serves as both owner and operator, thereby insuring consistency of service and quality.

Situated on 12 beautiful acres, Wyndham Roanoke Airport projects a mini-resort appearance in the middle of considerable urban activity. Catering to both the business and leisure traveler, Wyndham offers the best of both worlds: top quality business amenities, as well as leisure and family necessities.

The hotel features 320 guestrooms, many offering balconies with breathtaking mountain views. Health and fitness amenities include indoor and outdoor pools, full-service fitness center with sauna and whirlpool, lighted tennis courts, and nearby, an 18-hole golf course, horseback riding, hiking, and water sports. Wyndham also offers 12,000 square feet of flexible meeting space, including two ballrooms, four conference rooms, a director's suite with fireplace, and a conference theater.

At Wyndham, there is the belief that there is a right way to do things, called the Wyndham Way. It is reflected in the special treatment provided each guest, as well as in the casually elegant public areas and guestrooms. Thoughtful touches in guest rooms include coffee makers, shower massage, dataport and voice mail, individual climate control, in-room movies, hair dryers, Bath & Body Works toiletries, and a complimentary *USA Today* newspaper each morning.

Outstanding dining is also offered. Dining and entertainment also includes Charades, a lounge with music and satellite sports, and Whispers, the lobby lounge with fireplace, Lily's, a casual restaurant serving breakfast, lunch, and dinner, and, of course, Wyndham's first class room service.

However, Wyndham offers more than physical comforts. It takes great pride in being responsive to guests' needs. Whether those needs are business or pleasure, the Wyndham staff is dedicated to making certain that guests' stays are memorable. Dedicated meeting specialists are available to handle everything from intimate receptions to sophisticated multimedia productions. Additionally, since a growing number of business travelers are women, Wyndham established Women on Their Way, a special program focused on women. Wyndham representatives solicit advice from a women's advisory board and opinions from travelers via questionnaire to learn what appeals to the woman traveler.

The wedding day is also an important event to Wyndham and one that its experts have had considerable experience planning. Everything leading up to the ceremony and all that follows is perfectly orchestrated and flawlessly executed by the Wyndham. The hotel's easy-to-use Web site allows visitors to contact a consultant for detailed information, review of Wyndham's various honeymoon offers, and to choose from an extensive list of menu selections.

A four-point program has also been designed to ensure successful meetings. At Wyndham, understanding the meeting planner's objectives is the first and most integral step in ensuring a successful meeting. That is why Wyndham

THE WYNDHAM ROANOKE AIRPORT PROVIDES A PERFECT SETTING FOR MEETINGS, RECEPTIONS, AND TRAVELERS.

GUESTS CAN ENJOY UPGRADED AMENITIES IN THEIR GUESTROOM OR THROUGHOUT THE PICTURESQUE 11 1/2-ACRE FACILITY.

confirms the objectives in writing. This document, called "Wyndham's Meeting Partnership," is signed by the sales manager, the meeting services manager, and meeting planner. The customer's objectives become Wyndham's objectives, and they are communicated throughout the organization.

Also, for meetings of all sizes, Wyndham offers a special number, 1-888-Wyndham.

Both business and leisure travelers can appreciate the frequent flier partners program. Wyndham provides guests with frequent flier miles from a variety of airline partners, including American Airlines, Delta Air Lines, TWA, United Airlines, USAirways, Canadian Airlines, and Midwest Express.

In more than 150 spectacular destinations across North America and the Caribbean, Wyndham Resorts consistently sets standards for corporate and leisure travel. The hotel's policy is to treat guests as valued friends.

From the moment of check-in until departure, guests' comfort is the priority. That is in evidence with the "By Request" program, which starts with a personal profile that can be completed on line (www.wyndham-byrequest.com), by mail, or by phone (toll-free 1-800-994-2227).

Wyndham keeps this information on file at its hotels and customizes the clients' rooms each day with beverages, snacks, reading materials, and special features previously requested. This program also features no registration, airlines miles, an automatic 2 p.m. checkout, an upgrade to the best available room or suite available, travel assistance, and a toll-free member service center.

It is all available with a call to the toll-free number or a visit to the Web site, www.wyndham.com. ∎

BERGLUND AUTOMOTIVE GROUP

As the Number One Chevrolet dealer in Virginia, Berglund has been setting industry standards for the past 30 years. They have sold more new cars and trucks during the past five years than any other Chevy dealer in Virginia, as confirmed by Virginia Department of Motor Vehicle registrations. Berglund has also been voted the Roanoke Valley's best auto dealership for the past two years by the readers of the *Roanoker Magazine*.

Berglund is the only certified Five-Star Jeep dealer in the Roanoke Valley. Berglund has achieved Jeep's most prestigious dealer award by demonstrating a commitment to value and customer service. Five-Star recognition is the highest award that Jeep can give a dealership and requires dealers to provide a customer-focused sales and service experience by following a strict set of training, facility, and employee requirements.

As testimony to Berglund's impressive customer service, they have received numerous service awards in addition to their notable Five-Star rating. Among them are recognition as a GM Service Supremacy Dealer and AAA approval of both the service and body divisions. Berglund's service technicians are factory certified, 30 percent of which are at the master level. The company was also the first dealer in Virginia to offer GM Mobile Service to customers. Berglund takes customer satisfaction very seriously.

The Berglund Automotive Group consists of three distinct businesses. Berglund Chevrolet Jeep Buick on 1824 Williamson Road in Roanoke offers sales, service, leasing, parts, and body shop. Berglund Ford Pontiac Mazda provides sales, service, leasing, and parts to Salem from its location on 834 Main Street. Berglund Outdoors is a creative recreation station, offering customers travel trailers, pop-up campers, Polaris ATVs, fifth-wheels, personal watercraft, and Victory motorcycles. Also, motor homes and pop-up campers can be rented. Berglund Outdoors is located in Cloverdale on 2590 Lee Highway, Route 11.

Berglund has based their reputation on providing customers with some of the most innovative services in the automotive market. For example, Berglund recently announced a new interactive Web site, www.berglundcars.com, which features customer-friendly car-buying tools.

The site furnishes everything the purchaser needs to buy a car in one place. It loads quickly, navigates easily, and provides the tools for researching and purchasing a vehicle.

The site allows customers to:
- Check insurance rates and even purchase insurance directly;
- Purchase any Ford, GM, or Chrysler part directly;
- Search and view Berglund's entire new and used inventory;
- Apply for special license plates;
- Find interest rates and calculate loan payments;
- Connect to all manufacturers' sites; and
- Check new and used car values on Kelley Blue Book or NADA official guides.

Berglund's service department also stays abreast of the latest techniques and the leading-edge tools, equipment, and processes. Berglund emphasizes supporting their technical service and support staffs by providing on-going training both on site and at certified factory schools. By doing this, Berglund leads the way with today's highly technical and rapidly changing cars and trucks. The company uses the latest technology to assist in identifying problems and tracking and maintaining quality control of the repairs.

Additionally, customers purchasing new and used cars from Berglund receive their customer support services. When a new vehicle is bought, the customer receives a Loan-A-Car every time the vehicle needs warranty repair. Most other dealers require overnight repair work in order to get a loaner. At Berglund, customers get a Loan-A-Car even if the repair work takes only one hour. Berglund has invested more than $2 million in a fleet of 90 Loan-A-Cars. The vehicles are available to customers, so they are not inconvenienced by warranty repair work.

Berglund has a huge selection of used cars, most every make and model, but customers can be assured that Berglund does not sacrifice quality for quantity. Each of these cars is carefully inspected and is of the highest quality. Over 300 trade-ins every month fail Berglund's strict mechanical/safety check and are sold to other dealers. The used vehicles at Berglund are the best of the best. That is why Berglund can afford to include a 12 month, 12,000 mile powertrain warranty on every used vehicle they sell. This is not an extended agreement for which the customer pays, but an added benefit all Berglund used-car buyers enjoy.

Berglund's commitment to customers doesn't stop there. It extends to the entire community. The Berglund Foundation was created to support the community and make donations to a variety of groups and individuals in the Roanoke Valley.

Berglund has received the Leadership Award for contributions to the United Way of the Roanoke Valley. The Berglund Foundation has donated vehicles to the Roanoke Valley American Red Cross and the Roanoke City Police Department for community outreach programs. Berglund is especially proud to play an important part in the development of youth soccer in the Roanoke Valley, promoting physical well-being, teamwork, social interaction with other children, and encouraging youth to set personal and team goals.

Berglund's slogan, "You Can Count On Us," is reflected in a record of success and growth, cutting-edge information systems, community involvement and support, and renowned customer service efforts. Berglund's 300-plus employees are driven by dedication to their customers and their community. Customers can count on Berglund for a great selection, friendly employees, quality service, and a lower price, every time. ∎

BERGLUND HAS A HUGE SELECTION OF USED CARS, MOST EVERY MAKE AND MODEL, BUT CUSTOMERS CAN BE ASSURED THAT BERGLUND DOES NOT SACRIFICE QUALITY FOR QUANTITY. EACH OF THESE CARS IS CAREFULLY INSPECTED AND IS OF THE HIGHEST QUALITY.

BERGLUND IS ESPECIALLY PROUD TO PLAY AN IMPORTANT PART IN THE DEVELOPMENT OF YOUTH SOCCER IN THE ROANOKE VALLEY, PROMOTING PHYSICAL WELL-BEING, TEAMWORK, SOCIAL INTERACTION WITH OTHER CHILDREN, AND ENCOURAGING YOUTH TO SET PERSONAL AND TEAM GOALS.

FIRST TEAM AUTO MALL

First Team Auto Mall is the ninth offspring of Bill Lewis Chevrolet Corporation of Portsmouth-Chesapeake, reflecting the success of 50 years of steady growth. Throughout the years, First Team has strived to be the preferred automotive dealership by employing empowered, motivated people responsible for producing an excellent purchase and ownership experience. This was the vision more than 50 years ago, and it is the vision today.

First Team Hyundai was opened in the fall of 1988. George R. Pelton, then vice president and general manager of Bill Lewis Chevrolet, moved to Roanoke and became president and dealer operator of First Team. They acquired the Suzuki franchise in 1989 and the Isuzu franchise two years later to become First Team Auto Mall. Then in 1994 the Nissan, Subaru, and Volkswagen franchises were added making First Team Auto Mall the largest import dealer in Virginia west of Richmond. And in 1999, First Team added the Daewoo franchise to their extensive line of vehicles offered.

First Team Auto Mall's track record for success and continued growth, innovative programs, and excellent customer service efforts have made it a leader, not just in the Roanoke area, but across the nation serving Virginia, North Carolina, Maryland, Pennsylvania, West Virginia, Texas, and Arizona. They have even delivered an Isuzu Trooper to Chile.

First Team Auto Mall has set an industry trend with its "No-Hassle" buying experience. George Pelton, president of First Team, says, "For too long people dreaded going to the dealer and buying a car. Additionally there was a great disparity of cost among genders. We simply decided to even the playing field. At First Team Auto Mall, our lowest price is clearly marked on the windshield of every vehicle and that price is the same for everyone."

First Team Auto Mall also strives to stay current on new technology. Their innovative Web site is continually updated and extends the "No-Hassle" experience to the comfort of home.

In addition to the "No-Hassle" price guarantee, First Team's service is exceptional. Service Department technicians, most of whom are factory Master level and ASE certified, continually receive updated training from factory schools and on-the-job training. The excellent service provided builds a strong relationship with customers and is evidenced by a large percentage of repeat business.

First Team Auto Mall not only provides for employees and customers, but also takes great pride in helping the community as well. Since 1992, First Team has been a major sponsor of the Roanoke Area Youth Substance Abuse Coalition (RAYSAC), providing a new vehicle each year for the raffle at the RAYSAC After Prom Party Grand Finale. In order to qualify for a chance to win the new vehicle, area high school juniors and seniors must attend their school's After Prom Party, pledge to stay alcohol and drug free for that night, and be chosen to represent their school at the Grand Finale event. Promoting awareness of the effects of alcohol and the problem of driving under the influence is a cause that hits close to home for the First Team family. In 1993, less than a year after beginning to sponsor the RAYSAC event, Mr. Pelton's son was killed by a drunk driver. In the years since, First Team, in conjunction with Hyundai Motor America, has established the Geoffrey Reed Pelton Memorial Scholarship that is presented each year at the After Prom Party Grand Finale. High school seniors compete for this scholarship by submitting an essay of their suggestions and ideas on how to eliminate driving under the influence and underage drinking.

First Team Auto Mall's mission is to build a continuing relationship with customers by providing a superior product and caring, trained personnel to make each experience at First Team a pleasant one. There are countless "thank you" letters received each month congratulating First Team personnel for providing clear, concise information and conducting business in an honest and courteous way.

Throughout the years consumer habits, attitudes, and needs have changed and will continue to change. First Team Auto Mall has evolved into one of the most successful

dealerships in Virginia because it has adapted its approach to customer needs and desires.

This well-respected Roanoke dealership has earned numerous awards and honors for exceeding goals in both sales and service. But the one area where it has truly excelled is in keeping its customers satisfied. ■

THIS WELL-RESPECTED ROANOKE DEALERSHIP HAS EARNED NUMEROUS AWARDS AND HONORS FOR EXCEEDING GOALS IN BOTH SALES AND SERVICE. BUT THE ONE AREA WHERE IT HAS TRULY EXCELLED IS IN KEEPING ITS CUSTOMERS SATISFIED.

FIRST TEAM AUTO MALL IS THE LARGEST IMPORT DEALER IN VIRGINIA WEST OF RICHMOND, WITH HYUNDAI, SUZUKI, ISUZU, NISSAN, SUBARU, VOLKSWAGEN, AND DAEWOO FRANCHISES.

VIRGINIA'S EXPLORE PARK

The vision of Virginia's Explore Park was conceived in 1985 by a number of community leaders wishing to create an anchor attraction that would teach visitors about the region's unique natural and cultural heritage, encourage environmental protection, create a diverse recreational venue, and stimulate western Virginia's economy.

THE FALLAM-BATTS EXPEDITION OF 1671 MARKED THE FIRST CONTACT WITH TOTERO PEOPLE LIVING IN THE ROANOKE VALLEY. INTERPRETERS AT VIRGINIA'S EXPLORE PARK RECREATE AN EARLY NATIVE AMERICAN VILLAGE.

FRONTIERSMEN WERE SCATTERED THROUGHOUT THE ROANOKE VALLEY IN THE MID-1700S. SETTLERS WORKED HARD TO BUILD TEMPORARY HOMES IN THE WILDERNESS.

Today, the realization of that dream, Virginia's Explore Park, is situated on 1,100 pristine acres in southeast Roanoke County along the Blue Ridge Parkway and bisected by the Roanoke River. Over 800 acres of parklands are designated natural areas and remain undeveloped. The park features a bevy of opportunities for leisure activity, learning, and fun.

The popular historic district is home to costumed interpreters who teach visitors about life in western Virginia from the pre-contact Native American to the colonial frontierspeople to the settlement of Virginia as we know it. A recent addition to the 19th century area includes a working batteau on the Roanoke River, highlighting river culture during that era and the life of the freed African-American slave. An upcoming addition to the historic district is the 1850s Slone's Grist Mill, a recent acquisition from Franklin County that is being carefully reassembled by the historic structures staff and is expected to open in 2001.

Botetourt County's own 1880s Mountain Union Church rests on a bluff overlooking the historic district and is a popular facility for weddings, concerts, and town meetings.

For the outdoor enthusiast, the park features a number of recreational opportunities, including six miles of hiking trails, 10 miles (and growing, thanks to a dedicated core of volunteer trail builders) of mountain biking trails, and canoeing, kayaking, and fishing in the Roanoke River.

To complement the daily programming, Explore Park hosts a number of special events including the Blue Ridge Garden Festival, Subaru Bike and Outdoor Festival, Appalachian Folk Festival, and Native American Pow Wow, as well as scholarly conferences on such issues as watershed protection and historic and cultural preservation.

Visitors enter Virginia's Explore Park by way of the Roanoke River Parkway, a 1.5-mile spur road from the Blue Ridge Parkway. The Arthur Taubman Welcome Center is located at the terminus of the Roanoke River Parkway and serves as a gateway for park visitors and a rest station for weary Parkway motorists wanting a respite from their travels or to shop at the Rawanoke Trading Company. The Welcome Center also serves as a mini-conference center, offering rental space for meetings, receptions, and special events.

Adjacent to the Welcome Center is the historic Brugh Tavern restaurant, where diners can enjoy a delicious meal in an upscale, historic ambience.

The Blue Ridge Parkway Visitors Center—a cooperative venture between the National Park Service, Roanoke County, and Virginia's Explore Park—is being constructed between the Arthur Taubman Welcome Center and the Brugh Tavern. The mission of this 9,600-square-foot facility is to chronicle the history of the Blue Ridge Parkway and highlight the communities along its corridor.

Construction of the envisaged world-class Hancock-Cartledge Education Center, which will be built in the same development area using sustainable technologies and will serve as an adjunct facility for on-site programming, will begin in the near future.

Virginia's Explore Park has remained a popular destination for school groups. The park's historic and environmental education programs are uniquely designed to meet the Commonwealth's Standards of Learning for public schools, which means a day at the park is like a day in the classroom, only more fun!

Virginia's Explore Park receives funding from state and local governments and from the private sector, including individuals, corporations, foundations, gate receipts, and retail sales. It is a unique public-private partnership between The River Foundation, a not-for-profit foundation and founding entity, and the Virginia Recreational Facilities Authority (VRFA), which is managed by a 13-member board of directors appointed by the governor. The River Foundation and VRFA have enjoyed a productive relationship since inception.

Roger Ellmore, executive director of Virginia's Explore Park, explains, "Most people in Roanoke take the mountains for granted. Many don't realize that mountains are the second most popular tourist destination and the scenic Blue Ridge Mountains are no different. We look at this land as a canvas onto which every group has painted a different story. So whichever track you take at this park—a walk through history, a ride on the river, or a cycle on the mountainside—there's a good chance of finding something outside the ordinary to enjoy."

Explore Park's future is bright indeed as buildout of this exciting destination attraction continues. The board of directors and staff are committed to providing western Virginia residents and visitors to the region with a first-class attraction focused on its mission to meet the needs of the region well into the 21st century. For more information, call (800) 842-9163 or visit Virginia's Explore Park's web site at www.explorepark.org. ∎

BY 1850, MANY FARMSTEADS DOTTED THE WESTERN VIRGINIA COUNTRYSIDE. SAMUAL HOFAUGER AND ELIZABETH HAYS HOFAUGER RAISED FOUR CHILDREN IN THIS HOME ONCE LOCATED ON COLONIAL AVENUE IN ROANOKE COUNTY.

FESTIVALS AND SPECIAL EVENTS ARE HELD THROUGHOUT THE YEAR AT VIRGINIA'S EXPLORE PARK FEATURING MUSIC, CRAFT DEMONSTRATIONS, AND REENACTMENTS.

LEE HARTMAN & SONS

Lee Hartman & Sons, a family-owned business headquartered in Roanoke, has been selling and performing service on sophisticated sound systems, televisions, and audiovisual equipment since 1936. Three generations of Hartmans work together keeping abreast of developments in the electronics field and offering the latest technology coupled with unsurpassed service to their customers, both residential and commercial.

Lee Hartman Jr., president of Lee Hartman & Sons, explains, "The secret to our success and continued growth is diversity. We are a general electronics store, rather than a specialty store. We do not specialize in one particular product, but provide a wide array of most innovative products for both home and business. We complement this horizontal growth with our depth of knowledge and service."

Comprehensive, individualized service sets Lee Hartman & Sons apart from its competitors. The sales and support staffs are highly trained to ascertain the individual needs of each customer and put together a system that meets each particular need. From concept to completion, Lee Hartman & Sons provides turnkey audio/video systems to customers in Virginia, West Virginia, Kentucky, Tennessee, Maryland, North Carolina, and Florida. Throughout these states, Hartman's markets span residential and commercial organizations, including hospitals, educational facilities, television stations, conference centers, resorts, and corporate boardrooms. Although the financial backbone of the company is realized in retail sales and sound system installation, it also maintains a strong presence in the audiovisual rental arena, performing service for both residential and commercial customers.

Lee Hartman & Sons takes pride in providing the finest service and products designed to give the customer long-term value. From cellular phones to plasma televisions, the company carries a complete line of products to match customer needs for quality, performance, and price. In addition, Hartman provides a wide array of communication equipment, consumer and professional sound equipment, stage lighting and special effects, teleconferencing equipment, consumer and professional computer equipment, audio and video duplication, conversion of foreign videotapes to NTSC, and custom-designed home theaters.

Lee Hartman & Sons offers a wide selection of audio visual equipment at its retail location in Roanoke, as well as an extensive catalog and detailed Web site, which features monthly specials and detailed information on the latest products available to enhance corporate communications or home entertainment.

Whether you are planning a new or renovated boardroom, auditorium, training facility, conference room, production area, broadcast room, or home theater, Lee Hartman & Sons can create an audio visual system that will address specific requirements efficiently and cost-effectively. It designs tailored solutions based on the specific needs of each customer application. Lee Hartman & Sons not only installs the equipment, but also follows up to refine the system and offers on-going technical service and support.

Although Lee Hartman & Sons has a strong presence throughout the Eastern U.S., it continues to lend its support to many regional and local organizations, such as Mill Mountain Theatre, First Night Roanoke, Virginia Military Institute, Fishburn Academy, and area fund-raising endeavors and charitable causes.

Lee Hartman & Sons employs 48 people at its Roanoke facility, four of which are family members. Officers of the company include: Lee Hartman Jr., president; Jack L. Hartman, vice president; Cathleen Hartman, secretary treasurer; Steve Hartman, general manager; and Virginia Norcross, serving as assistant secretary treasurer.

A strong field sales force complements the company's main staff. Its employees are long-term because, as part of its mission, Lee Hartman & Sons pledges to provide employees with a good economic standard of living and an interesting and pleasant work environment. This goes hand in glove with the company's commitment to provide its customers with high-quality products and comprehensive, on-going service.

Lee Hartman & Sons understands the ever-increasing role that technology plays in the world today. It also understands that it is critical that schools and businesses be able to use the latest in audio-visual equipment to meet their communication and production goals. That is why Lee Hartman & Sons plans to continue its long tradition of focusing on its expertise in providing the best and most economical solutions to both the worldwide home and the worldwide corporate communities.

"There's much more to come in the high-tech world of the future," Hartman says. "We've only just begun to scratch the surface with what we can provide to our customers in both convenience and state-of-the-art communication capability." ■

VIRGINIA NORCROSS, ASSISTANT SECRETARY TREASURER.

CATHLEEN HARTMAN, SECRETARY TREASURER AND FOUNDER, WITH JACK L. HARTMAN, VICE PRESIDENT.

THE KROGER CO.

In 1883 Barney Kroger opened his first grocery store in Cincinnati, Ohio, and named it the Great Western Tea Company. Two years later he had four stores and The Kroger Co. grocery chain was born.

Over the next 20 years, Kroger's chain grew steadily and by 1902, he had 40 stores and a factory in Cincinnati. The name was then changed to Kroger Grocery & Baking Company, and the dynasty began.

During this time, Barney Kroger became a pioneer in food advertising, taking out newspaper ads almost as large as the grocery advertisements of today. He also drew attention and customers by maintaining prices lower than all his competitors. His strategy was quite innovative for its time: attract customers to the store by running a large ad in the newspaper and sell out a carload for a small profit on each item. Although this is commonplace in today's merchandising market arena, at the time it was revolutionary.

As more expansion and innovation continued, The Kroger Co. became the first food chain in the nation to operate bakeries and the first to incorporate meat departments in grocery stores.

Kroger also took advantage of motorized transport to spread the organization throughout the Midwest. In the 1920s, the firm bought out smaller chains in geographic areas adjacent to existing Kroger operations.

In August of 1929, The Kroger Co. took its first step into the foothills of the Blue Ridge Mountains and the great Shenandoah Valley with the purchase of 92 Jamison stores and 7 Piggly-Wiggly stores spread over portions of Virginia, Tennessee, West Virginia, and North Carolina. Regional headquarters for the division were established on the second floor of the company's warehouse on Norfolk Avenue at Henry Street. In 1937, the warehouse and headquarters moved to Shenandoah Avenue and, in 1959, new facilities were completed.

In 1974, the Roanoke division merged with the Charleston, West Virginia, division to become the Alleghany marketing area and later the Mid-Atlantic marketing area.

Then, in 1983, Mid-Atlantic marketing area officials moved Kroger's regional operations from the Glenvar warehouse into a new headquarters on Peter's Creek Road in the City of Roanoke.

The Mid-Atlantic marketing area now operates 137 stores; 12 of them in the Roanoke Valley, and employs more than 14,000 people in Virginia, West Virginia, North Carolina, Tennessee, Kentucky, and Ohio.

The Kroger Co.'s growth continued in the Roanoke Valley with its "Store of the 1990s" introduced in 1988 featuring a 55,193-square-foot food and drug combination. This particular concept met the ever increasing needs of customers to save time and experience one-stop shopping.

As it continues to be known as the supermarket of choice, Kroger has increased its strong presence in Virginia by acquisitions. These acquisitions included stores in Lynchburg, Roanoke, Lexington, Farmville, Blacksburg, Appomattox, Waynesboro, Richmond, and Hampton Roads.

As the nation's largest supermarket retailer, Kroger maintains its high standards of customer service, quality products, and community involvement. Kroger continues to gain market share because of its reliable, dependable, convenient service to the customer. By continually exceeding the needs of the consumer through innovation and quality service and product, The Kroger Co. remains positioned to succeed in the changing world of the future. ∎

KROGER'S NEWEST PROTOTYPE STORE MEETS TODAY'S BUSY CONSUMER'S NEEDS BY OFFERING A ONE-STOP SHOPPING EXPERIENCE.

LEE & EDWARDS WINE MERCHANTS

Wine and fine cuisine are a part of gracious living for many. In past years, the selection of quality, value-oriented wines as well as fine vintage bottlings in southwest Virginia was marginal. No longer does the enjoyment of the diverse world of wine and cuisine require a search beyond this region to other markets.

F. Lee Tucker solved that dilemma in November 1995 (on the day of the release of Beaujolais Nouveau—the first wine of the new vintage year) by opening Lee & Edwards Wine Merchants in downtown Roanoke.

With a lifelong interest in wine, winemaking (enology), and wine-grape growing (viticulture), he co-founded the first wine festival in southwest Virginia, the Smith Mountain Lake Wine Festival in 1989. Then, inspired by the availability and selection of fine wines found in the dedicated wine shops of Manhattan and London, Tucker envisioned a premier wine and craft beer retail establishment in Roanoke.

Locating in downtown Roanoke because of the availability of historic structures amenable to renovation, Tucker personally directed the renovation of the circa 1910 building, that is now home to Lee & Edwards, with sensitivity to the original design. A reproduction tin ceiling 14 feet overhead exactly matches the original. He was the recipient of the Golden Trowel Award in 1996 in recognition of the effort.

As a collector of fine wines, Tucker understood the importance of proper storage conditions. As a result, incorporated into the renovation was a temperature- and humidity-controlled wine cellar. The temperature is maintained at 55 to 60 degrees Fahrenheit and humidity at 70 to 75 percent. Fine wines and champagnes rest under ideal conditions until they are sold.

An eclectic interest in cuisine is evident in the wide selection of international foods at Lee & Edwards. An attendee of the International Fancy Food Show in New York, the owner regularly returns with the best of the show to Roanoke.

If Lee & Edwards has a mission, it is to make the enjoyment of wine and gourmet food accessible to anyone with an interest. The knowledgeable staff teaches customers to trust their own palates. The store's cruvinet wine sampling system allows customers to evaluate a wine first-hand. Tasting programs are tailored to the novice, as well as the expert. In-store wine and food tastings are held on Saturdays. Once a month, the "First Tuesdays" tasting is an informational wine tasting with a theme where wines are paired with compatible food specialties. Lee & Edwards sponsors periodic wine dinners with an international emphasis at area restaurants.

Downplaying the snob-appeal of fine wine, the offerings definitely indicate that good wine doesn't have to be expensive. Tucker and his staff research, taste, and select every wine, especially value-oriented wines that are less well known to the public. For the aficionado, the cellar is packed with an international inventory of the best vintages. Virginia wines are well represented and Lee & Edwards' comprehensive selection has resulted in annual award recognition.

With Lee & Edwards' entry into the Roanoke Valley market, there is no longer the need to travel to D.C. or New York to find wines of high quality. ■

ABOVE: THE JEFFERSON STREET ENTRANCE TO LEE & EDWARDS WINE MERCHANTS DOWNTOWN ROANOKE.

LEFT: DEPTH OF SELECTION AND PERSONALIZED SERVICE ARE HALLMARKS OF THE LEE & EDWARDS SHOPPING EXPERIENCE.

ENTERPRISE INDEX

Adelphia Business Solutions
111 Franklin Road, Suite 110
Roanoke, Virginia 24011
Phone: 540-342-5070
Fax: 540-342-2221
E-mail: absresponse@adelphiacom.com
www.adelphia.com
Page 123

Adelphia Communications
21 South Bruffey Street
Salem, Virginia 24153
Phone: 540-389-6750
www.adelphia.com
Page 122

Allstate Insurance Company
1819 Electric Road, SW
Roanoke, Virginia 24018
Phone: 540-989-2200
Fax: 540-989-2670
www.allstate.com
Pages 140-141

The Atlantic Mutual Companies
1325 Electric Road, SW
Roanoke, Virginia 24018
Phone: 540-989-3300
Fax: 540-989-5994
www.atlanticmutual.com
Page 146

Berglund Automotive Group
1824 Williamson Road
Roanoke, Virginia 24012
Phone: 540-344-1461
Fax: 540-343-8404
E-mail: roanokecci@berglundcars.com
www.berglundcars.com
Pages 176-177

The Branch Group, Inc.
PO Box 4004
Roanoke, Virginia 24022
442 Rutherford Avenue, NE
Roanoke, Virginia 24016
Phone: 540-982-1678
Fax: 540-982-4217
E-mail: ralphs@branchgroup.com
www.branchgroup.com
Pages 154-155

Carilion Biomedical Institute
117 Church Avenue
Roanoke, Virginia 24011
Phone: 540-581-0123
Fax: 540-581-0125
E-mail: blanar@carilion.com
www.biomedicalinstitute.com
Page 127

Carilion Health System
1212 Third Street
Roanoke, Virginia 24016
Phone: 540-981-7641
Toll-free: 800-422-8482
www.carilion.com
Pages 164-165

Dragon Chemical Corporation
7033 Walrond Drive
Roanoke, Virginia 24019
Phone: 540-362-3657
Fax: 540-362-5762
Page 125

The Egg Factory
2840A Hershberger Road
Roanoke, Virginia 24017
Phone: 540-777-6095
Fax: 540-777-6555
E-mail: innovate@eggfactory.com
www.eggfactory.com
Page 126

First Team Auto Mall
6520 Peters Creek Road
6900 Peters Creek Road
Roanoke, Virginia 24019
Phone: 540-366-4830
Fax: 540-563-1252
www.firstteamautomall.com
Pages 178-179

The Glebe
250 Glebe Road
Daleville, Virginia 24083
Phone: 540-992-6711
Toll-free: 877-994-5323
Fax: 540-992-2973
E-mail: theglebe@rbnet.com
www.vbh.org
Page 170

**Harris Office Furniture
Company Inc.**
520 Kimball Avenue, NE
Roanoke, Virginia 24016
Phone: 540-344-5549
Fax: 540-342-9521
Page 147

**Hayes, Seay, Mattern &
Mattern, Inc.**
1315 Franklin Road, SW
Roanoke, Virginia 24016
Phone: 540-857-3100
Fax: 540-857-3180
E-mail: hsmm@hsmm.com
www.hsmm.com
Pages 138-139

Hill Studio
120 West Campbell Avenue
Roanoke, Virginia 24011
Phone: 540-342-5263
Fax: 540-345-5625
E-mail: davidhill@hillstudio.com
Page 145

ITT Industries
7635 Plantation Road
Roanoke, Virginia 24019
Phone: 540-563-0371
Fax: 540-366-9015
E-mail: nvsales@itt.com
www.ittnightvision.com
Pages 120-121

The Kroger Co.
3631 Peters Creek Road
Roanoke, Virginia 24019
Phone: 540-563-3500
www.kroger.com
Page 184

Lanford Brothers Company, Inc.
122 North Commerce Street
PO Box 7330
Roanoke, Virginia 24019
Phone: 540-992-2140
Fax: 540-992-2139
E-mail: ken@lanfordbros.com
www.lanfordbrothers.com
Pages 152-153

**Lawrence Transportation
Systems**
872 Lee Highway
Roanoke, Virginia 24019
Phone: 540-966-4000
Fax: 540-966-4555
E-mail: sales@lawrencetransportation.com
www.lawrencetransportation.com
Page 133

Lee & Edwards Wine Merchants
309 South Jefferson Street
Roanoke, Virginia 24011
Phone: 540-343-3900
Fax: 540-343-4116
E-mail: lande@rev.net
Page 185

Lee Hartman & Sons
3236 Cove Road, NW
Roanoke, Virginia 24017
Phone: 540-366-3493
Fax: 540-362-4659
E-mail: lhartman@leehartman.com
www.leehartman.com
Pages 182-183

Martin & Associates
5007 Carriage Drive
Roanoke, Virginia 24018
Phone: 540-989-9700
Fax: 540-989-4405
E-mail: m4design@rbnet.com
Page 144

National Financial Services, Inc.
4401 Starkey Road
Roanoke, Virginia 24014
Phone: 540-989-4600
Fax: 540-989-0169
E-mail: hearp_eddie@nlvmail.com
www.nfservicesinc.com
Pages 142-143

North Cross School
4254 Colonial Avenue, SW
Roanoke, Virginia 24018
Phone: 540-989-6641
Fax: 540-989-7299
www.northcross.org
Page 166

Oakey's Funeral Service & Crematory
318 Church Avenue
Roanoke, Virginia 24016
Phone: 540-982-2100
Fax: 540-344-9625
E-mail: oakeys@roanoke.infi.net
www.oakeys.com
Page 169

Optical Cable Corporation
5290 Concourse Drive
Roanoke, Virginia 24019
Phone: 540-265-0690
Fax: 540-265-0724
E-mail: kharber@occfiber.com
www.occfiber.com
Pages 124

Roanoke County
5204 Bernard Drive
Roanoke, Virginia 24018
Phone: 540-772-2006
Fax: 540-772-2193
www.co.roanoke.va.us
Pages 158-159

Roanoke County Schools
5937 Cove Road
Roanoke, Virginia 24019
Phone: 540-562-3920
Fax: 540-562-3994
E-mail: lscarhorough@rcs.k12.va.us
www.rcs.k12.va.us
Pages 160-161

Roanoke Higher Education Center
108 North Jefferson Street
Roanoke, Virginia 24016
Phone: 540-767-6000
Fax: 540-767-6020
E-mail: info@education.edu
www.education.edu
Page 167

Roanoke Regional Airport
5202 Aviation Drive, NW
Roanoke, Virginia 24012
Phone: 540-362-1999
Fax: 540-563-4838
E-mail: rrac@roanokeairport.com
www.roanokeairport.com
Page 134

The Roanoke Times
PO Box 2491
Roanoke, Virginia 24010
201 West Campbell Avenue
Roanoke, Virginia 24010
Phone: 540-981-3211
Toll-free: 800-346-1234
www.roanoketimes.com
Pages 130-131

Salem Veterans Affairs Medical Center
1970 Roanoke Boulevard
Salem, Virginia 24153-6478
Phone: 540-982-2463
Fax: 540-983-1096
www.va.gov
Pages 162-163

The Spectacle Lens Group of Johnson & Johnson Vision Care, Inc.
5568 Airport Road
Roanoke, Virginia 24012-1311
Phone: 540-362-2020
Fax: 540-362-2050
Pages 116-119

Town of Vinton
311 South Pollard Street
Vinton, Virginia 24179
Phone: 540-983-0607
Fax: 540-983-0621
E-mail: vintondb@aol.com
Page 168

Virginia's Explore Park
Milepost 115, Blue Ridge Parkway
PO Box 8508
Roanoke, Virginia 24014
Phone: 540-427-1800
Fax: 540-427-1880
E-mail: lsadler@explorepark.org
www.explorepark.org
Pages 180-181

WSLS, Newschannel 10
401 Third Street, SW
Roanoke, Virginia 24011
Phone: 540-981-9110
Fax: 540-981-2189
www.wsls.com
Page 132

Wyndham Roanoke Airport
2801 Hershberger Road, NW
Roanoke, Virginia 24017
Phone: 540-563-9300
Fax: 540-561-7910
E-mail: kgeorge@wyndham.com
www.wyndham.com
Pages 174-175

BIBLIOGRAPHY

1996 Economic/Education Impact Study of the Roanoke Region's Cultural Industry. Roanoke, Virginia: Arts Council of the Blue Ridge, 1997.

1998 Community Plan. Roanoke County, Virginia: Roanoke County Planning Department, 1998.

Arts Council of the Blue Ridge: 1999 Annual Report. Roanoke, Virginia: Arts Council of the Blue Ridge, 2000.

Art Museum of Western Virginia: Spring 2000. Roanoke, Virginia: Art Museum of Western Virginia, 2000.

Cultural Directory. Roanoke, Virginia: Arts Council of the Blue Ridge, 1999.

Kagey, Deedie. *When Past is Prologue: A History of Roanoke County.* Marceline, Missouri: Wadsworth Press Inc., 1988

Kagey, Deedie. *When Past Was Prologue: A History of Roanoke County.* February, 2000.

Roanoke County Demographic and Economic Profile. Roanoke County, Virginia: Roanoke County Planning Department, 1996.

Roanoke Valley of Virginia, 2000 Visitors' Guide. Roanoke, Virginia: Roanoke Valley Convention and Visitors Bureau, 2000.

The Roanoke Valley of Virginia, 2000 Visitors' Guide. Salem, Virginia: RP Publishing Company, 2000.

A Statistical Guide to the Roanoke Metro Area. Roanoke, Virginia: Roanoke Regional Chamber of Commerce, Small Business Development Center, 1998.

White, Claire. *Roanoke 1740-1982.* Roanoke, Virginia: Hickory Printing, 1982

Other Resources
City of Roanoke: www.ci.roanoke.va.us
City of Salem: www.ci.salem.va.us
County of Roanoke: www.co.roanoke.va.us
The Hotel Roanoke & Conference Center: www.hotelroanoke.com
Optical Cable Corporation: www.occfiber.com
Roanoke Regional Airport: www.roanokeairport.com
Roanoke Regional Chamber of Commerce: www.roanokechamber.org
The Roanoke Valley Convention & Visitors Bureau: www.visitroanokeva.com
Roanoke Valley Resource Authority: www.rvra.net
Roanoke Wildlife Rescue: www.roanokewildlife.org

PHOTO BY LINDA A. TURNER.

ACKNOWLEDGEMENTS

The publisher and authors would like to thank the following people who contributed information to this book:
Sara Bemiller, Mill Mountain Theatre
John Coates, Roanoke City Department of Parks and Recreation
Louise Garman, farmer, Catawba
Teresa Thomas Gereaux, Public Relations Director, Roanoke College
Pete Haislip, Roanoke County Parks and Recreation Department Director
Ginny Henderson, farmer, Back Creek
Susan Jennings, Director Arts Council of the Blue Ridge
Dr. James Sears, Center in the Square
Matt Miller, Fifth Planning District Commission
Phil Sparks, Director Roanoke Valley Economic Development Partnership
Wayne Strickland, Director of Fifth Planning District Commission
Joyce Waugh, Roanoke County Department of Economic Development

The publisher and authors would like to thank the following people who contributed photography to this book:
Fran Ferguson, Center in the Square
Jim Hubbard, Roanoke Valley Resource Authority
Beth Pullin, Roanoke Symphony Orchestra

Contributing Photographer
Tommy Firebaugh
   Tommy L. Firebaugh is a professional photographer residing in the Roanoke, Virginia, area. He has been a member of the Virginia Professional Photographers Association (VPPA) since 1986 and has been voted "Best Area Photographer" by the readers of the *Roanoker Magazine* eight of the last nine years. In addition to winning awards in local and regional arts and crafts shows, his work has been collected in numerous restaurants and businesses all over the world. Many of his works hang in private residences.

Profile Writers
Judy Siegel
   Judy Siegel, president and founder of Blue Sky Marketing, has 20 years experience in marketing, advertising, creative writing, and public relations.
   Currently a free lance writer and editor, she has written articles for newspapers, magazines, and businesses throughout the country specializing in women's health, sports, and education. Her collection of poetry, *Between the Lines*, won her national acclaim.
   She resides in Blacksburg, Virginia, with her husband, Dr. Marc Siegel, her son Matthew, and their two golden retrievers.

Sharon Gnau
   Sharon Gnau is a Roanoke-based freelance writer, whose day job is at Mill Mountain Theatre. She is a graduate of Hollins University in communications and is a native of Austin, Texas. She is the mother of two girls.

Contributing Profile Writers
Laurel Holder
Amy L. Shelor
Christina Koomen Smith

A special thanks to the Celebrate 2000 Photo Contest Judges:
Dr. Norma Jean Peters
Dr. Robert Sulkin
Dr. Elizabeth Heil
Stephanie Klein-Davis

PHOTO BY PETE LARKIN.